The Faithful Finisher

Walking With the God Who Transforms Faders Into Finishers

Bonnie Jean Schaefer

Dream Doers Publishing LLC

CONTENTS

WHY THIS BOOK EXISTS

I had just finished the 101 Day Triple Crown Challenge — 101 consecutive days of writing a children's story, publishing a podcast episode, and running or walking a mile. Every. Single. Day.

I proved I could finish an ambitious mission. I became diligent. Disciplined. Someone who showed up and did what she said she'd do regardless of how she felt.

And then I looked at what I'd created: over 100 children's stories sitting in my digital files with no plan for what came next.

I turned to the shelf where my published novels sat. Three complete Dragon Stalker books. The fourth and final one of the series outlined but not written.

So many stories started. So few finished.

Then without the constraints of that challenge, I felt myself slipping back into old patterns. Starting new projects. Drafting more stories. Creating without publishing. Working without finishing.

I needed a bigger mission. Something that would force me to publish books, not just draft them. Something with three aspects like the challenge I'd just completed, but more focused on the transformation I actually needed and reaching the people my books could help.

That's when God laid the 50 by 50 Challenge on my heart: publish 50 books, complete 50 10Ks, and transform 50 lives by the time I turn 50.

I was about to turn 48. Two years to complete what seemed impossible.

And to make it audacious, I decided nothing from the past would count. No carryovers. No shortcuts. Just a clean slate and a grand adventure.

Fresh start. Focused mission. Two years to become someone who finishes faithfully.

But I had no idea how to get it done. I could see the milestones. I could picture the finish line. But the path? Unclear.

I knew this much: **worldly productivity systems weren't enough**. I'd tried them all. They got me to 80%, then left me stranded.

If I was going to finish this mission, I needed to model God and design my finishing strategies based on His character, not human systems.

The real mission wasn't about books, races, or impact metrics. It was about *becoming* — becoming someone who finishes what she starts.

Because if I couldn't learn to finish faithfully, I'd spend the rest of my life starting projects and abandoning them just before the breakthrough. I'd waste the gifts God gave me. I'd teach the kids I'm raising that dreams don't matter and finishing is optional. And I'd miss the transformation that only comes when you push through the final 10-20% where obedience costs the most.

God finishes what He starts. Every time. Without exception.

So I needed to understand the God who planned redemption before the foundation of the world, worked for 4,000 years without quitting, and finished the work of salvation through Christ on the cross even when every human emotion screamed for Him to stop.

This book is that journey. It's a deep dive into God's character as the Faithful Finisher. It explores what drives Him, how He plans, how He works, and how He completes everything He begins.

Because when I understand that God's faithfulness guarantees His finishing, I can ground my certainty in His character instead of my willpower.

What This Book Is Not

This book won't give you a productivity system. No time management hacks. No goal-setting frameworks. No 30-day challenge to transform your life.

What you will find is a theological exploration of God's character as the Faithful Finisher and an honest wrestling with what it means to become like Him.

If you want tactics without transformation, close the book now.

But if you're tired of trying harder and ready to become different — if you're done with surface-level solutions and willing to let God kill what needs to die so resurrection can come — then keep reading.

This is going to cost you something.

Why I Write Like I'm Talking to God

I don't need another system. I need God.

I needed to understand the God who never quits, never abandons His plans, and always sees His mission through to the end. Because if I'm going to become a faithful finisher, I can't rely on willpower. I need God's character transforming mine.

And transformation happens in conversation with Him, not in lectures about Him.

That's how I process truth. When I journal, when I pray, when I wrestle with hard questions, I talk them through with God. So instead of writing explanations about God's finishing nature, I wrote conversations with God. Instead of academic theology, I wrote prayers. Instead of self-help formulas, I wrote worship.

You're listening in on my talks with God about His vision, His strategy, His work, and His completion of the greatest adventure in history: redemption. You're overhearing someone wrestling with, wondering about, and worshipping the God who worked for roughly 4,000 years to prepare the world for Christ and then finished the work of salvation on the cross.

This book is designed to be a catalyst for your own prayers, a launching pad for your own exploration of how God finishes and how you can become a faithful finisher, too.

This book is for Christians — new or seasoned — who struggle to finish what they start or who finish but feel empty at the end. It's for dreamers who fear that success will pull them from God. It's for those who've convinced themselves their dreams don't matter. And it's for anyone ready to discover that finishing isn't about performance but fellowship with the God who transforms us through the work He calls us to do.

If you're exploring faith for the first time or want practical application before theology, start with the Gospel of John. Then come back to this book to discover how the life and ministry of Christ fits into God's grand design.

How to Experience This Book

Each chapter unfolds as a prayer, an authentic conversation with God about His character as the Faithful Finisher. Here's how to get the most from it:

Don't rush. This is a long conversation about character transformation, not a weekend workshop on time management. Each chapter explores profound truths about God's character that deserve time to penetrate your heart and mind. Give yourself space to absorb, reflect, and wrestle.

Make it your own prayer. Since every chapter is written as prayer, don't just read it. Pray it. Let my words spark your words. Let my struggles surface your struggles. Let my discoveries about God's finishing nature ignite your own conversation with Him. This isn't meant to be consumed passively. It's meant to provoke you into your own wrestling match with God.

Insert your own story. I write from my experience as someone who fades at 80-90%. But your story might be different. Maybe you finish but feel empty. Maybe you've stopped dreaming altogether because you're afraid of what success might cost. Wherever you are, make these conversations between you and God about who He is and how knowing Him in this way applies to your unique journey.

Get brutally honest. I confess my fears, my faulty beliefs, and my resistance to finishing throughout this book. I name the giants I'm fighting. I expose the lies I've believed. I almost deleted them before sharing them here to preserve my privacy. But I wanted you to see the real me so perhaps you could find the courage the see the real you. So don't skip over the hard parts. Sit with them. Ask God to show you what needs to die in you so that Christ can live more fully through you. This isn't comfortable work. It's crucifixion work. And crucifixion hurts.

Expect resistance. The closer you get to finishing this book, the more you'll be tempted to quit. (I had to fight through resistance to finish writing and revising it!) That's spiritual warfare in action. The enemy doesn't want you to become a faithful finisher because faithful finishers are dangerous. They accomplish what God calls them to do. So when you hit 80% and want to abandon this book, remember that's exactly where the transformation happens.

My Heart for You

I want to finish what I start so that I experience deeper fellowship with the God who finishes. And I want everyone who reads this book to discover what I'm discovering: finishing isn't about willpower. It's about walking with the God whose character guarantees completion.

My prayer is that these conversations don't merely teach you how to finish projects but transform you into someone who finishes faithfully because you're becoming more like Christ. I pray that you discover what took me years to understand: the invisible mission (Christlikeness) always matters more than the tangible mission (the book, the business, the body).

When you truly encounter the Faithful Finisher, you'll discover that finishing isn't the death of purpose but the gateway to new assignments. You'll learn that completion creates capacity. You'll understand that God cares more about who you're becoming in the process than what you're accomplishing at the end.

And you'll realize that the God who planned redemption before the foundation of the world, worked for 4,000 years to prepare the world for Christ, and finished the work of salvation on the cross through Christ is the same God who's finishing the work He started in you.

He will complete what He begins.

Including transforming you into a faithful finisher.

The God who never quits is waiting to show you how to finish like He does.

Let the conversation begin.

Opening Prayer

Dear Father,

I remember that day about a decade ago. Sitting at my desk. Reading the story of David and Goliath. Marveling at David's faith. Realizing the source of his faith: YOU.

He knew You. That's why he could face that giant and win.

When everyone else saw an impossible battle, David declared, "You come against me with a sword, spear, and javelin, but I come against you in the name of the Lord of Armies, the God of the ranks of Israel — you have defied Him. Today, the Lord will hand you over to me" (1 Samuel 17:45-46a).

David's knowledge of Your character and his surrender to Your authority enabled him to stand before that giant with certainty. He saw and did what no one else dared because he knew You.

That's when I understood that knowing is the starting point of success.

Paul knew this. "My goal is to know Him and the power of His resurrection and the fellowship of His sufferings, being conformed to His death" (Philippians 3:10).

That's why I wrote *The Only I AM* and *The King Who Befriends*. I wanted to consolidate my understanding of who You are and how You relate to me.

Now I need to understand what You want, why, and how You get it.

Because chasing my dreams isn't about accomplishing great things. It's about experiencing life with You in a way that allows You to work through me to show Yourself creative, loving, powerful.

I have big dreams burning in my heart, and I've been afraid to pursue them. I don't have the resources, certifications, education, status, or relationships the world says I need.

Good.

If I had the "right" qualifications, I'd trust my own strength instead of Yours. I wouldn't be able to point to You and say, "Look at who God is! This is the God who made you and wants to do great things through you, too."

But I have a giant standing between me and my dreams.

My Goliath isn't a literal giant daring me to fight. My giant is a conglomeration of doubts, misbeliefs, and inaccurate thinking about who I am in You and what You're able to accomplish through me.

Through this book, I want to face my giant and finish what I start the way You do.

I ask You to refine me as I pray through this book. I know my circumstances won't be different by the time I write the final word, but I want to be drastically different in the way I think, in the way I feel, and in the way I understand who You are and what drives You.

Show me the essence of Your character that makes finishing inevitable for You. Show me the complete pattern You follow:

- How You **DREAM** from Your character that fuels Your driving desire.

- How You **DO** the work with persistent action, never quitting despite obstacles.

- How You **REAP** the rewards of redemption You planned before time began.

Teach me this 3-Phase Follow Through so I can finish like You finish. Not just crossing finish lines, but completing the entire transformation from who I am now to who You're calling me to become.

Because I've been stopping too soon. I DREAM. I DO. But I don't REAP. I finish tasks but abandon the harvest. I cross finish lines but skip the transformation.

So show me how to follow through all three phases. Show me what desires and dreams derive from Your character, how You turn those dreams into goals and plans, how You work Your plan, how You follow through and win, how You celebrate and rest, and how that finishing creates capacity for what comes next.

Help me walk through that whole process. Help me understand how to model Your character and Your process so that I can live a well-done life for the praise of Your glory.

To do that, show me my enemy first. The doubts and misbeliefs that stand in the way of living fully and completely for Your glory.

"Search me, God, and know my heart; test me and know my concerns. See if there is any offensive way in me; lead me in the everlasting way" (Psalm 139:23-24).

Give me an honest heart. A repentant heart. Help me not drench myself in shame or regret but face what I've been thinking, feeling, believing so I can see it clearly and accurately.

Help me see You clearly and accurately so I can align my thoughts, feelings, and actions with Your truth. Most of all, align my dreams and desires with Yours because that motivation drives everything else.

That requires surrender.

Father, to completely surrender to You, I have to know what I need to surrender. Show me what I'm holding onto. What has become a stronghold in my life. What is keeping me small. What is keeping me from knowing You the way You want to be known and experiencing You the way You designed our relationship to be.

Help me put off these ineffective beliefs and put on truth. "Take off your former way of life, the old self that is corrupted by deceitful desires, to be renewed in the spirit of your minds, and to put on the new self, the one created according to God's likeness in righteousness and purity of the truth" (Ephesians 4:22-24).

Show me what stones to pick up and put in my sling to slay this invisible enemy. Help me fight with the truth of who You are. Give me an accurate view of You, an accurate view of me, and an accurate view of the world around me.

"Do not be conformed to this age, but be transformed by the renewing of your mind, so that you may discern what is the good, pleasing, and perfect will of God" (Romans 12:2).

Help me renew my mind day after day so I can finish well. Help me be a faithful servant and faithful steward of all You entrust to me — my time, my talents, my treasures, my relationships, everything.

Expose my weaknesses so I can replace them with Your strengths. You told Paul, "My grace is sufficient for you, for My power is perfected in weakness" (2 Corinthians 12:9).

Transform me from a sporadic fader into a faithful finisher who walks with You through every phase of the journey: DREAM, DO, and REAP.

In Christ,

Amen

1

LIVING AN ALMOST DONE LIFE

DEAR FATHER,

You say to cast all my cares on You, because You care for me. "Casting all your cares on Him, because He cares about you" (1 Peter 5:7). I believe You. I believe You do care, and I believe You are more than capable of bearing my burdens and solving my problems.

And my problem is this: I start lots and lots and lots of projects, but I finish few of them. Of those I do finish, I experience an empty sense of achievement at the finish line and lose all sense of direction and purpose and motivation that got me there in the first place.

Why is that, God? Why do I struggle to finish what I start?

At my job, I execute with excellence. I show up. Set targets. Do the work. Finish. Then repeat. Day after day. Week after week. Month after month. Year after year. Being an employee is practical. Logical. Predictable. I know what's expected, and I deliver.

But when it comes to my dreams as an entrepreneur — writing, speaking, marketing — I struggle. I start strong. I work hard. Then I fade before or right at the finish line despite knowing how to execute effectively.

Something inside of me is broken, and the only way to fix it is to seek You, not another goal-setting system or productivity hack. You. Because when You start something, You finish it. Always. Without fail.

So when You want something, how do You plan for it? How do You work the plan? How do You finish?

What does finishing look and feel like? How do You even decide what You want in the first place?

When I wanted to understand the essence of Your character and attributes, You showed me who You are as the Only I AM.

When I wanted to understand how You relate to me and vice versa, You showed me who You are as the King Who Befriends.

Now I want to understand what You want, why, and how You get it, so please show me who You are as the Faithful Finisher so that I can finish faithfully, just like You.

The First Fading Finish

December 2, 2001. The Raleigh Marathon.

For sixteen weeks, I trained. I pushed through the heat. I ran in the rain. I conquered distances I never thought possible: nine miles, then thirteen, then fifteen, then eighteen, then twenty, then twenty-two.

I registered. I paid the entrance fee. I showed up at the starting line with thousands of other runners, all of us with numbers pinned to our shirts and timing chips attached to our shoelaces.

I looked like a runner. But inside, I knew the truth: I was just pretending.

Didn't the people around me know I didn't belong? They'd know when the race began. They'd pass me and laugh and wonder why I was trying to be something I had never been before, something I couldn't be that day.

The starting gun exploded, and I surged forward with the crowd. People on the sidewalks clapped and yelled and cheered. My parents waved me onward at mile two and mile four. When I ran beyond their gaze, sight of each mile marker inspired me to find the next. Every water station felt like a gift from heaven.

At mile 13.1, I was ahead of pace. My breathing was normal. My cadence was steady. I waved to my parents with sweaty confidence. Even if I took a little longer to run the second half, I'd still finish in my self-imposed goal of four hours and thirty minutes. I'd even be able to sprint the final stretch like I had always imagined.

But at mile 15, my feet started complaining. Both knees added their protests. My muscles refused to maintain the pace.

Until mile 17 appeared. Tears of joy filled my eyes at the sight of that blessed number. I was making progress after all.

The pain hovered just beneath my skin throughout the next six miles. Up hills. Down hills. Around curves. I was running so slow I feared I would never find the end. *And sprinting the final stretch? What a fantasy. I would consider it a win to cross the finish line on my hands and knees.*

But the sight of the 23rd mile marker spurred me on. Only three miles left. Then two. Then one. I was almost done.

A strange sensation vaporized my pain. My feet and knees and muscles banded together for one last burst. I passed other weary runners. The crowd noticed. They called out my number. I sprinted faster.

The finish came into view.

A few more yards.

A few more feet.

Done.

I was done. It took me four hours and thirty-one minutes — ninety seconds over my goal— but I was done. My impossible dream of running a marathon just became a memory.

With the crossing of that finish line, I started to believe that everything I ever imagined accomplishing was indeed possible.

I knew it all along, but I had to run to make myself believe it.

The Emptiness at the Finish Line

But something strange happened in the days after.

The passion. The excitement. The thrill.

All gone.

Vanished.

Zapped away.

How did I go from feeling like anything was possible to not being sure I ever wanted to run again?

The nagging reality of missing my goal time made me believe I wasn't the runner I thought I had become.

I had crossed the finish line. I had proven I could do what I once thought was impossible. But instead of celebrating the victory, I felt empty. Like all the work leading up to that moment was worthless because I missed my time goal by ninety seconds.

Besides, thousands of other people finished that marathon, too. More than half of them finished ahead of me. The way I saw it, I didn't do anything special or important by finishing that marathon, and I lost all drive to keep running and training after that. It took years to find it again.

What I Didn't Understand About Finishing

I thought finishing meant crossing the finish line. I thought once I hit 26.2 miles, I was done.

I was wrong.

You showed me through creation that finishing is a COMPLETE PROCESS that involves debrief, rest, and reaping rewards, not just task completion.

DREAM → DO → DEBRIEF → REST → REAP REWARDS

I didn't debrief to evaluate who I'd become in the process and assess the quality of my effort the way You evaluated the quality of Your work after finishing each day of creation. I didn't rest intentionally the way You did when Your work of creation was complete. And I didn't let myself reap the rewards of a job well done the way You were able to reap the rewards of creation by walking with Adam and Eve in the garden.

So I couldn't dream again at the level of who I became as a result of finishing the marathon.

That's why I feel like a fader. Not because I quit the work. But because I quit the finishing process before it was complete.

I finished the TASK but not the TRANSFORMATION.

After the marathon, I should have debriefed: "I ran 26.2 miles. I proved the impossible is possible. I became tougher, more disciplined, more dependent on You. I AM a runner now."

I should have rested: Intentional recovery time, not sporadic, purposeless running.

I should have reaped rewards: "This is a victory worth honoring. Ninety seconds over my goal doesn't diminish what I accomplished."

Then I would have been ready to dream again from my new level: "Now I can pursue that four-hour marathon goal. Now I can train for another marathon with confidence."

But I didn't complete the cycle after that first marathon. So I couldn't access the transformation.

It took years and three other unfulfilling marathons before I could effectively dream again, do the work, and hit that four-hour marathon goal. When I finally crushed it with a 3:46 finish, something different happened. I felt complete. Satisfied. Done. Not empty like the others. Truly finished. I haven't felt the need to run another marathon since. That phase of my athletic life was over, and I could move on without regret.

But I didn't understand WHY that fifth marathon felt different. I stumbled into completion without knowing what I'd done. So the fading pattern kept showing up everywhere else in my life.

Why Do I Sabotage the Finishing?

When I published my first novel after nearly a decade of writing and rewriting, it fell flat. Instead of celebrating the accomplishment of finishing a publishable book, I focused on the poor sales and lost all motivation.

My second novel sold thousands of copies, but I didn't know what to do with that taste of success. I didn't evaluate, celebrate, or rest. So I let the momentum fade. I still haven't finished the fourth and final book in that series I started more than twelve years ago.

During that time, I've left a trail of almost-finished writing projects in my wake including training books for authors and over 100 children's stories that I drafted but never published.

Year after year, I start with hope for grand possibilities. But I tend to dream too big, and by September or October, I realize there's no way I can do all I set out to do. So my motivation fades. I scratch the year and figure next year will be better. Each time I start over, I feel a mix of regret for unfinished goals and excitement for new possibilities.

But what's it like to finish a year strong, evaluate what I learned, celebrate the victories, rest intentionally, and THEN plan the next year from who I've become? What's it feel like to be certain that I'll finish the entire cycle the way You do?

The Real Problem Beneath the Pattern

You've opened my eyes so that I can now see what the real problem is, Father.

I equate winning with selfish ambition and vain conceit.

I know pride is my greatest weakness, and I worry that if I go after impossible dreams and achieve them, I'll believe I won in my own power, get cocky, and forget You. Plus I don't want to let myself think that winning is going to fill my human needs for fulfillment, significance, and belonging because You are the only One who can satisfy the deep desires of my heart, the desires You placed in me that point me to You.

My burning desire is to know You and experience You and depend on You, and I always find You in the process. I always find You in the struggle, in the hard, when I'm doing the things that seem impossible because that's when You shine the brightest in me.

And yet I don't believe my dreams matter. I don't believe I'm supposed to win. I've trained myself to believe that dreams are a fun bonus in life, that they keep life interesting, but they're dessert, not the main course mission. So I never let myself finish the transformation from dreamer me to dream doer me.

I've decided other people can live their dreams, but I can't. I'm stuck being an employee and believe my business will always be a hobby despite how big my dreams are. I believe I'm doomed to normalcy, not greatness.

Finishing the entire cycle feels dangerous. If I evaluate honestly, I'll have to acknowledge I'm becoming someone capable of greater things. If I celebrate, I'll have to admit the victory matters. If I rest, I'll have to trust You're still with me even when I'm not striving.

So I fade before those final steps and keep myself small. That keeps the hope alive that someday maybe my dreams will come true while never actually letting them transform me.

I've been finishing in only TWO phases:

- **DREAM** ✓ (I know my character, desires, and dreams.)
- **DO** ✓ (I plan, work, and sometimes cross finish lines.)
- **REAP** ✗ (I skip the debrief, rest, and rewards.)

I thought finishing meant completing the DO phase — crossing the finish line, declaring the task done, moving on to the next thing.

But You're showing me finishing means following through to REAP the rewards. That's the part I've been abandoning. The harvest I've been leaving in the field.

I've been a Dream Doer who stops before the REAP phase. And without reaping, there's no transformation. No new capacity. No higher floor to dream from next time.

That's why I feel like a fader. I finish tasks but not the whole process. I cross finish lines but abandon the follow-through.

The 101 Day Challenge: Finishing Without Transforming

I do know what it's like to finish the way I dream and plan, though.

I was certain I would finish the 101 Day Challenge before I started because I decided to follow through no matter what. You prepared me for the mission and enabled me to fight through any obstacle. I walked with You every day for those 101 days as I wrote a children's story, published a podcast episode, and ran or walked a mile. I became someone who showed up and did what I said I was going to do regardless of how I felt.

I followed all the way through to the end of the action, but I didn't intentionally debrief or rest or reap any rewards. Because after I finished the work, none of the work I did seemed all that important.

I didn't see any tangible rewards from 101 days of action. I saw a stack of stories, a string of podcast episodes, and 101+ miles that contributed to feeling fit, diligent, and disciplined, but I didn't see any value in anything I created. Besides, who really cared besides me and You?

The 101 Day Challenge proved I could finish when I commit. But it exposed my fading problem. I completed the DREAM phase. I executed the DO phase faithfully — all 101 days. But I skipped the REAP phase entirely.

I didn't debrief to extract the wisdom. I didn't rest intentionally before starting the next thing. I didn't reap the rewards by celebrating who I'd become and solidifying my new identity as someone who shows up regardless of how I feel.

Without that final phase, the transformation never settled. I finished the task but stayed the same person who just accomplished something instead of becoming someone new with greater capacity.

When I realized months later that finishing the work isn't enough, I asked You for a mission that would force me not just to cross finish lines, but to follow through all the way to REAP the harvest. To complete the entire 3-Phase Follow Through: DREAM → DO → REAP.

The Impossible Mission

That's what the 50 by 50 Challenge is really about.

The 50 by 50 Challenge — publish 50 books, complete 50 10Ks, and transform 50 lives by the time I'm 50 — is a wild ambition. But it's a purposeful one.

I want to have a total of 50 books published by the time I'm 50 (in less than two years as of this writing) because I already have that many books and stories started in various stages of creation. Finishing them will clear the creative runway so that I can finally finish the epic conclusion of the Dragon Stalker series.

I'm aiming for 50 10Ks that I run, walk, bike, or hike because I want my body to stay as strong as my faith on this journey. Maintaining the 6.2-mile endurance level keeps me physically disciplined for the creative race ahead. Although the 10k distance is easy for me and won't stretch my physical limits the way that a half-marathon or marathon would, the purpose of this 50 by 50 mission isn't to push my physical limits; it's to push my creative and leadership limits. So the 10Ks keep me consistent and active while I race forward in these other areas of my life, especially as I do the hardest thing of all — invite other people into this journey.

I'm asking You to bring 49 others into my world who want to learn what I'm learning about living for You because transformation multiplies. I am the first of those 50 lives I want this mission to change, and I don't want to change alone.

But to effectively help others, I need to change first. I need to transform from a fader into a finisher.

The Empowering Solution

Lord God, You never struggle as a fader the way I have described here. You always finish what You start. Always. You always know exactly what to do, when, why, and how. You always follow through at precisely the right time in the most effective way.

You don't just finish the TASK. You complete the entire DREAM – DO – REAP process.

And each completion prepares the way for what comes next.

"I am sure of this, that He who started a good work in you will carry it on to completion until the day of Christ Jesus" (Philippians 1:6). You don't abandon what You start. You see it through all three phases — DREAM, DO, and REAP.

Because You always have a plan.

"I declare the end from the beginning, and from long ago what is not yet done, saying: My plan will take place, and I will do all My will" (Isaiah 46:10).

You planned the world before You made it. You planned redemption before sin was even a problem. You even planned me before I was born.

You are the GOAT — Greatest of All Time — of following through. You DREAM. You DO. You REAP. The complete 3-Phase Follow Through.

I want to be like You. I want to learn from You how to DREAM from godly character, DO the work my dreams require with persistent faith, and REAP the rewards the work produces. After all, You planned, executed, and finished the grandest adventure the world has ever seen with the project of redemption.

So please teach me to follow through like You. The whole process. Not just crossing the finish line, but completing the entire transformation from who I am now to who You're calling me to become.

However, I can't understand how You dream, work, or reap until I dig deep into understanding Your faithful and finishing nature.

2

THE FAITHFUL FINISHER

DEAR FATHER,

Before I can learn to finish like You, I need to see who You are as the Faithful Finisher. Reveal Your character. Show me that finishing flows from who You are, not what You have or accomplish.

It is Your character that guarantees You will finish. Your dreams and plans flow from Your unchanging, eternal, sovereign nature. Your work is sustained by Your power. And Your completion is certain because You cannot fail.

I want to understand this character-based guarantee. What does it mean that You are faithful? What does it mean that You're a finisher? What evidence do You provide of both?

What Faithful Means

When I think of faithfulness, I think of reliable. Certain. Consistent. Steady. Loyal.

You are utterly dependable. "Because of the Lord's faithful love we do not perish, for His mercies never end. They are new every morning; great is Your faithfulness!" (Lamentations 3:22-23).

I can trust You to be who You have revealed Yourself to be and to do everything You have promised to do. You are reliable and worthy of my trust.

You remain consistent with Your holy, just, loving character and promises across all of time and in all circumstances.

"Know that the Lord your God is God, the faithful God who keeps His gracious covenant loyalty for a thousand generations with those who love Him and keep His commands" (Deuteronomy 7:9).

Your loyalty doesn't depend on my performance but on Your character.

Your faithfulness is the foundational reality that makes all other faithfulness possible. "God is faithful; you were called by Him into fellowship with His Son, Jesus Christ our Lord" (1 Corinthians 1:9).

My faith in You rests in Your faithfulness. Your faithfulness describes the kind of finisher You are.

What Finisher Means

As a Finisher, You begin with the end in mind. You maintain faithfulness throughout. You work from power rather than willpower. You evaluate completion against an immovable standard so that You know what done looks like. And You rest when the work is done, completed, finished.

Faithful is a character attribute — who You are. Finisher is a role identity — what defines You.

I can't yet claim the role or identity of finisher, but You can. And I want to be like You.

"Keeping our eyes on Jesus, the source and perfecter of our faith. For the joy that lay before Him, He endured the cross, despising the shame, and sat down at the right hand of the throne of God" (Hebrews 12:2).

As the source and perfecter of my faith, Jesus is the One who begins, leads the way, and brings everything to completion. He starts and ends everything.

Jesus doesn't just finish things sometimes, complete tasks, and demonstrate a strong work ethic. I can say that of me, but Jesus is so much more.

Jesus finishes. This is His nature, a role, an identity. He is a Finisher.

In other words, Jesus doesn't fade. He follows through to the end. Every time.

Like Jesus, You don't fade. You finish. You reach the goal. Every time. You complete Your purposes. Every time. You accomplish Your mission. Every single time.

Your character guarantees You finish what You start. Your power ensures that nothing will stop You. Your purpose ensures You what You finish matters.

You don't ask me to trust You without solid evidence. So You provide both Your general revelation and Your special revelation to show me that You do indeed finish what You start.

And not just finish the task — You finish the COMPLETE CYCLE.

Creation: The Fast and Snappy Finish

I don't have to look very far in scripture to find evidence of Your finishing nature. In Genesis 1-2, You started with nothing and ended with an entire universe.

You demonstrated Your faithfulness by showing up in the same way day after day. You spoke. Your words became reality. You assessed what You made. You declared what You made good. You always evaluated the work You did. That evaluation signaled the end of each day.

You never needed any do-overs. Nothing You created was incomplete or sub-par. "God saw all that He had made, and it was very good indeed" (Genesis 1:31). It was all good the first time.

Day 7 was different, though. You took a whole day to rest.

"On the seventh day God had completed His work that He had done, and He rested on the seventh day from all His work that He had done. God blessed the seventh day and declared it holy, for on it He rested from all his work of creation" (Genesis 2:2-3).

It couldn't have been because You were tired because You don't get tired. You set apart that seventh day to celebrate the creative work You did and establish a pattern of finishing well.

You worked with focus and fire for six days, then gave Yourself a day off to set a pattern for me: work hard, finish well, evaluate, rest, repeat. You blessed the day of rest because the work was done.

All the work You did during those first six days was intentional and organized. You didn't create man before land or the sun before the sky. Nor did You create chaos like trees that couldn't grow, birds that couldn't fly, or fish that couldn't swim. You made everything just right the first time.

When it was all done, You declared it very good, gave Yourself the reward of rest, and blessed the completion. You FINISHED everything You set out to create.

This teaches me that finishing matters to You, You evaluate completed steps along the way, and that You rest rather than diving straight into the next project. You also let Yourself experience the rewards of Your work. These rewards include enjoying the beauty of a wondrous creation that sings Your praises and the fellowship of people made in Your image to reflect Your glory.

You work in this way not because You need to go step by step...but because I do. You model the way You designed me to work — in cycles of transformation.

I've been finishing tasks but not finishing cycles. I cross the finish line, then immediately start something new without evaluating, resting, or reaping the rewards I've earned.

That's why I feel like a fader. I'm dreaming, planning, working, and sometimes following through. But I'm skipping the final 10 - 20% — the debrief, rest, and reaping rewards parts that actually complete the transformation.

And I wouldn't see any of this if I didn't have Your word to show me who You are.

So instead of stopping at Your general revelation and having people wonder who designed them and where they came from and why, You embarked on another project to share Your specific revelation with us through Your word.

The Bible is yet more evidence that You faithfully complete what You start.

Scripture: The Slow and Diligent Finish

You worked diligently to reveal Yourself to us through the written word over the course of about 1500 years. You used 40 authors to write 66 books that tell ONE story. Your story. The story of who You are, how You redeem us from our sin through Christ, and what is still to come. The Bible is no longer an ongoing project. It's a COMPLETED work.

"I testify to everyone who hears the words of the prophecy of this book: If anyone adds to them, God will add to him the plagues that are written in this book. And if anyone takes away from the words of the book of this prophecy, God will take away his share of the tree of life and the holy city, which are written about in this book" (Revelation 22:18-19).

Your revelation about Yourself is complete. No more books. No additions. No updates or amendments or editions needed. The canon is closed. When You were done speaking in that unique way, You stopped.

The process You used to write this book that is still alive and powerful today is unique. You revealed Yourself little by little, and by the end, we have a complete picture of everything we need to know about You to choose whether or not to serve You.

"Long ago God spoke to the fathers by the prophets at different times and in different ways. In these last days, He has spoken to us by His Son. God has appointed Him heir of all things and made the universe through Him" (Hebrews 1:1-2).

In the past, You spoke through prophets and apostles. Now You speak through Christ and His completed work. You don't need to add anything because You finished what You set out to communicate about Yourself.

"All Scripture is inspired by God and is profitable for teaching, for rebuking, for correcting, for training in righteousness, so that the man of God may be complete, equipped for every good work" (2 Timothy 3:16-17).

I am thoroughly equipped. Not partially. Not almost. THOROUGHLY. Because Your Word is COMPLETE.

I start projects and abandon them at 80%, if I get that far. But You started Scripture and saw it through to the end. 100% DONE. I'm always adding to my plans or starting new projects before I finish the old. But You completed the canon and made it clear that nothing should be added or deleted.

This teaches me that You finish what You start, even if it takes more than a thousand years. You don't rush. You don't leave anything incomplete. You finish in Your way and in Your time. You work patiently, thoroughly, and completely. Nothing is missing from scripture that is necessary for me to know, and nothing is included that is unimportant or extra or unnecessary.

Redemption: The Progressive and Powerful Finish

You finished creation and are still working today to sustain what You created.

You finished Scripture and are still working today to preserve what You wrote.

And Scripture tells the story of redemption that You planned, worked, and finished through the death, burial, and resurrection of Jesus despite countless obstacles along the way.

Sin broke fellowship. Satan opposed Your plan. Humans failed repeatedly. But You finished anyway through Christ. And because You are faithful, reliable, and trustworthy, You are still working today to sustain what You created, preserve what You wrote, and sanctify Your children.

As a result, the Holy Spirit is working in me to help me overcome the power of sin and remain in a right relationship with You.

So when You promise to bring to completion the work You started in me, I can trust You to finish it.

"Now may the God of peace Himself sanctify you completely. And may your whole spirit, soul, and body be kept sound and blameless at the coming of our Lord Jesus Christ. He who calls you is faithful; He will do it" (1 Thessalonians 5:23-24).

You don't get bored or lose interest or abandon Your work. Because faithfulness is part of Your unchanging nature. You are the God who never leaves things undone.

This teaches me that I have Your power in me to fight through any obstacle and finish whatever I start with confidence and conviction because You are working in me. One day my sanctification will be complete, and I will at last be glorified and free from sin's presence forever.

You Are the Faithful Finisher

Finishing isn't just something You do. It's WHO You are.

You didn't just finish creation and stop. You created the world, then began preparing it for Christ.

You didn't just finish preparing and stop. You sent Christ to accomplish redemption.

You didn't just finish redemption and stop. You sent the Spirit to complete the transformation.

Each finished work led to the next mission. Each completion created space for what comes next.

You're showing me that finishing isn't the end of purpose. It's the gateway to new assignments.

And because You finished creation, Scripture, and redemption, my certainty shouldn't come from my willpower which fades, but from Your character, which never changes.

So how do I ground my dreams in who You are and what You want instead of who I am and what I want?

By walking with You through the story of redemption.

I want to see what drives You, how desires become dreams, how dreams become plans, and how plans become reality.

So what do You want and why? What is Your vision? What is the dream You've been pursuing since before the beginning of time?

There's something You want.

Something You're working toward.

Something that drives every finished work.

And I long to understand it. Because if I'm going to align my dreams with Yours...

If I'm going to treat my 50 by 50 Challenge the way You treat Your mission to sanctify me...

If I'm going to become a faithful Finisher like You...

Then I need to know what You are finishing for.

Show me Your mind. Show me Your heart. Show me the vision that fuels Your relentless follow through.

3

THE LOVING VISIONARY

DEAR FATHER,

As a holy, self-existent, eternal being, You need nothing and no one. You are complete in and of Yourself. The Trinity — Father, Son, and Spirit — exists in perfect fellowship for all eternity. You lack nothing.

So what do You want?

I'm not talking about the practical, tactical, tangible targets like creation, scripture, or redemption. I'm seeking an understanding of the motivational force behind those dreams.

Because dreams don't appear from nowhere. They're shaped by desires. And desires flow from character.

Your character is the foundation. Your desire flows from that. Your dream takes shape from both.

So if I'm going to align my dreams and desires with Yours, I need to understand what drives You because of who You are.

The Character That Drives Everything

Before You want anything, You ARE something. Love.

"Dear friends, let us love one another, because love is from God, and everyone who loves has been born of God and knows God. The one who does not love does not know God, because **God is love**" (1 John 4:8, emphasis mine).

Love isn't a fleeting feeling You experience or something You do. It's who You are. It's Your essential nature. And love by its very nature is RELATIONAL. It gives. It shares. It creates space for others.

That understanding helps explain why You exist as the Father, Son, and Spirit in perfect, eternal fellowship. I can't explain how Your Trinitarian nature works, but I do know it means that You've never been alone. You've never been isolated. You've always existed in relationship, in communion, in face-to-face intimacy.

You are also HOLY. "Holy, holy, holy is the Lord God, the Almighty, who was, who is, and who is to come" (Revelation 4:8b).

You are completely set apart from sin. Pure. Righteous. Perfect in every way. You cannot tolerate sin in Your presence because sin is the opposite of everything You are.

And You are GENEROUS. You don't hoard Your life, Your glory, Your joy. You SHARE. You create. You give. Not because You need anything from what You create, but because generosity flows from love.

This is who You are: loving, relational, holy, generous.

And who You are determines what You want.

The Desire That Flows From Love

Before the beginning of time, You wanted to enjoy walking with people who are holy and blameless before You in love.

Not because You were lonely. The Trinity has perfect fellowship.

Not because You needed something. You are complete in Yourself.

But because LOVE SHARES.

Love creates space for others to experience what love already enjoys. Love invites. Love opens the door. Love says, "Come, walk with Me. Talk with Me. Know Me. Be known by Me."

That's what You want. Faithful fellowship.

"I will put My teaching within them and write it on their hearts. I will be their God, and they will be My people" (Jeremiah 31:33b).

You don't just want people to know ABOUT You. You want people to KNOW You. Walk with You. Talk with You. Experience life WITH You.

This is Your driving desire: faithful fellowship with people who are holy and blameless before You in love.

The Dream That Gives Shape to Desire

Who You are — Your character — determines what You desire.

A desire is the deep ache for something. It's the motivation, the fuel, the WHY.

A dream is what that desire looks like. It's the picture, the vision, the WHAT.

DESIRE + DREAM = VISION

Your desire for faithful fellowship creates a specific dream. And I can see that dream in two places: the beginning and the end of Your story.

In the Garden of Eden, before sin entered the world, I see what Your dream looks like.

You created a perfect world — light and darkness, sky and sea, land and vegetation, sun and moon and stars, birds and fish and animals. Everything in its place. Everything working together in harmony.

Then You created people in Your image. "So God created man in His own image; He created him in the image of God; He created them male and female" (Genesis 1:27).

Not robots programmed to obey. Not slaves forced to serve. But IMAGE-BEARERS capable of relationship, capable of choice, capable of walking with You in love.

And in that garden, You walked with Adam and Eve "at the time of the evening breeze" (Genesis 3:8).

The sun descending. Cool breeze rising. You walking through the garden You planted with Your own words, calling for the man and woman You formed from dust and breath.

Face-to-face conversation with no barrier between You.

This is faithful fellowship. Your driving desire. Walking with people who are holy and blameless before You in love.

No sin. No separation. Just You and Your people, together, forever.

I long for that type of friendship with You. Because something in me recognizes this is what I was made for. What we were all made for.

And sin stole it. Stole me away from You.

So You bought me back with the blood of Christ and then show me what happens at the end of Your story.

In Revelation, I see Your same dream. But this time it's perfected, completed, eternal.

"Then I heard a loud voice from the throne: 'Look, God's dwelling is with humanity, and He will live with them. They will be His peoples, and God Himself will be with them and will be their God. He will wipe away every tear from their eyes. Death will be no more; grief, crying, and pain will be no more, because the previous things have passed away'" (Revelation 21:3-4).

No more separation. No more sin to break fellowship. No more tears, death, or pain. Just You and Your people, face to face, forever.

"They will see His face, and His name will be on their foreheads. Night will be no more; people will not need the light of a lamp or the light of the sun, because the Lord God will give them light, and they will reign forever and ever" (Revelation 22:4-5).

We will see Your face.

Not metaphorically. Not symbolically. Not through a glass darkly.

FACE TO FACE.

The way Adam walked with You in the garden before the fall. The way You always wanted it to be.

This is the dream You've been working toward since before the foundation of the world. This is the motivational force behind every finished work. This is the vision that fuels Your relentless finishing.

DRIVING DESIRE: Faithful fellowship with people who love You.

DREAM: Walking face-to-face with holy, blameless people in eternal friendship.

VISION: God dwelling WITH humanity forever.

You finish everything You start so You can dwell with me forever.

But there is a problem. A massive, devastating problem that makes fellowship with You impossible.

Sin.

The Gap Between the Dream and Reality

The moment Adam disobeyed You, fellowship shattered. Sin broke the relationship You enjoyed with Adam and Eve in the garden because You cannot abide in the presence of sin. Your people were no longer holy and blameless. The walking stopped. The intimacy ended. Separation replaced fellowship.

"For all have sinned and fall short of the glory of God" (Romans 3:23).

Sin is the core obstacle that stands between You and what You want most: relationship with me. And it has an earthly consequence I cannot escape: death.

"The wages of sin is death" (Romans 6:23a).

And Satan makes this problem worse. He roams the earth doing his best to tempt me to sin and keep me from enjoying a relationship with You. "Be sober-minded, be alert. Your adversary the devil is prowling around like a roaring lion, looking for anyone he can devour" (1 Peter 5:8).

Sin broke fellowship. Satan opposes restoration. Your dream looks impossible.

You don't give up on Your vision, though. You don't abandon Your desire. You don't say, "Well, that didn't work. Better try something else."

Because You are the Faithful Finisher. And faithful finishers don't quit when obstacles arise.

So the question becomes HOW? How do You bridge the gap between the dream (faithful fellowship) and the reality (sin and separation)?

You have a plan. And I want to understand it. But first, I want to ensure my vision is aligned with Yours.

My Ultimate Vision: Faithful Fellowship

I've been afraid to go all in on chasing my dreams because I worry that I'll get cocky if I become a well-known author or depend on money instead of You if I become wealthy.

But when I dream from a place of desiring faithful fellowship and delighting in You, my heart is aligned with Yours.

I don't have to fear the pride and selfishness in my heart when my will is surrendered to Yours. This surrender to You is a daily, ongoing battle.

Because sin is still present in me. Satan is still at work trying to drive me away from You. But that doesn't mean I can't dream and dream big. It doesn't mean that my dreams are daggers meant to destroy my spiritual health.

It does mean I have to constantly vet my desires against Yours to ensure my motives for wanting to achieve my tangible targets are aligned with Yours.

It does mean that living for Christ is my solution. Surrendering to Your authority and allowing Your Spirit to work in me transform me day by day and enables faithful fellowship.

When I thus align my desires with Yours by longing for fellowship above achievement, my dreams change. They become invitations to walk with You, not tasks to prove myself to You or anyone else.

Every dream born from Your desire for fellowship becomes a path to knowing You on a deeper level. That's how I trust my desires flow from who You are rather than my selfish desires.

Which is why the 50 by 50 Challenge isn't about publishing 50 books. It's about finishing projects I've started and walking with You through it all.

The dream is faithful fellowship. The books are just a way to live that reality.

I see it now! This is **PHASE 1: DREAM**.

CHARACTER (who You are) fuels DRIVING DESIRE (what You want) which shapes the DREAM (specific vision):

Loving, holy, generous God → faithful fellowship → walking face-to-face with holy people.

Without this foundation, dreams feel selfish, uncertain, dangerous. I question whether they matter. I wonder if pursuing them will pull me from You. I sabotage before I even begin. And everything that follows becomes hollow: uncertain plans, meaningless work, empty victories.

But when the dream flows from godly character and aligns with Your desire for fellowship, the dream matters. The plans make sense. The work is fulfilling. The finish line becomes transformation.

Now that I understand Your ultimate vision and how my vision aligns with Yours, show me Your plan.

Because vision without strategy is just a wish. And You don't wish. You FINISH.

You don't just DREAM. You DO.

"I call a bird of prey from the east, a man for My purpose from a far country. Yes, I have spoken; so I will also bring it about. I have planned it; I will also do it" (Isaiah 46:11).

How do You bridge the gap between the dream and the reality? How do You turn faithful fellowship from an impossible dream into an accomplished fact?

Show me Your strategy, Father. Show me how You planned to restore what sin broke.

4

THE PERSISTENT DOER

DEAR FATHER,

You crafted a vision before the foundation of the world: faithful fellowship with people who are holy and blameless before You in love.

But sin broke that fellowship. Satan opposes restoration. The gap between Your dream and reality looks impossible to bridge.

And yet, You don't give up. You don't abandon Your vision. You execute that vision through strategic planning and persistent work.

Because You are the Faithful Finisher. And faithful finishers don't just dream. They PLAN. They WORK. They persist through every obstacle until the vision becomes reality.

Now that I understand Your CHARACTER (loving, holy, faithful) and Your VISION (faithful fellowship), show me how You planned to achieve it and how You worked that plan.

Show me PLAN and WORK, the first two movements of the DO phase.

Because vision without a plan is just a wish. And a plan without execution accomplishes nothing.

You don't wish. You don't just plan. You WORK. For as long as it takes.

The Strategic Plan

You had a plan. A strategic, brilliant, progressive plan to restore what sin broke.

"For He chose us in Him, before the foundation of the world, to be holy and blameless in love before Him. He predestined us to be adopted as sons through Jesus Christ for Himself, according to the good pleasure of His will, to the praise of His glorious grace that He lavished on us in the Beloved One. In Him we have redemption through His blood, the forgiveness of our trespasses, according to the riches of His grace that He richly poured out on us with all wisdom and understanding" (Ephesians 1:4-8).

Not a plan to force compliance. Not a plan to override human choice. But a plan to work through human history, human failure, and human faith to accomplish redemption.

You determined to send the Seed (Christ) to crush the serpent's head and restore fellowship through His sacrifice.

Before Christ came, You planned to reveal details little by little through the prophets so the world would recognize the Messiah when He came.

Before the prophets, You planned to establish the royal line through David so the Messiah would have the rightful claim to the eternal throne.

Before the royal line, You planned to reveal the depth of the problem through the Law so humanity would understand our inability to save ourselves.

Before the Law, You planned to choose one nation to carry the promise and demonstrate to the world that You alone are God.

That was the plan. Little by little revelation. Progressive clarity. One strategic step at a time toward the ultimate goal: Christ.

You saw the end from the beginning and worked from the beginning to the end.

This is the PLAN step — the strategic roadmap that turns vision into achievable milestones.

You didn't rush. You didn't skip steps. You laid out the entire journey before You began the work.

But planning without execution is worthless. So You did what faithful finishers do: You WORKED the plan.

The 4,000-Year Timeline

Four thousand years, Father (give or take a few hundred years).

That's 40 centuries. 1,461,000 days. 35,064,000 hours.

From Adam to Abraham: roughly 2,000 years of waiting. From Abraham to Christ: roughly 2,000 more years of preparation.

People were born, lived their entire lives, and died without ever seeing the promise of Genesis 3:15 fulfilled. Entire civilizations rose and fell. Empires came and went — Egypt, Assyria, Babylon, Persia, Greece, Rome. Kings reigned and were forgotten. Generations upon generations waited.

Children asked their parents, "When will the Messiah come?"

The parents answered, "I don't know. But God is faithful."

Their children's children asked. A hundred generations asked. They all died. Still waiting.

And You never quit. Never abandoned the plan. Never said, "These humans are too hard-hearted to walk with anymore."

You worked with relentless patience through ordinary people and extraordinary circumstances over time and through trials. Because You are not bound by time. You don't measure success in quarters or years or even decades.

You measure it in completion. And You were willing to work for 4,000 years to reap the reward of faithful fellowship.

Through One Man: Working Despite Failure

In those early centuries, sin exploded. What started as disobedience led to murder, then to wickedness so pervasive that every thought was evil continually.

Satan must have thought he was winning.

But You were working. Through Noah, You preserved the seed. Through the flood, You judged rebellion while showing mercy to those who believed.

When humanity rebelled again at Babel, centralizing to make a name for themselves apart from You, You didn't destroy them. You scattered them. You slowed the spread of evil and preserved a world where You could still be known.

Then out of all the scattered nations, You picked one man: Abram (who You later renamed Abraham).

"The Lord said to Abram: 'Go out from your land, your relatives, and your father's house to the land that I will show you. I will make you into a great nation, I will bless you, I will make your name great, and you will be a blessing. I will bless those who bless you, I will curse anyone who treats you with contempt, and all the peoples on earth will be blessed through you'" (Genesis 12:1-3).

And he went. Not knowing where he was going. Just believing You would fulfill Your promise.

You didn't choose him because he was perfect. He lied about Sarah. Twice. He took matters into his own hands with Hagar and Ishmael when he couldn't see how You'd fulfill Your promise to make him a great nation.

But You worked through his failures. You stayed faithful when he wasn't. And You did what only You could do: You enabled Sarah to give birth to Isaac when she was 90 years old.

Through Abraham's family — seventy people who went down to Egypt during a famine — You multiplied them into more than 2 million by the time Moses was born.

Revealing the Problem Through the Law

Satan tried to wipe out the line through Pharaoh's command to kill Hebrew baby boys.

But You preserved Moses through Pharaoh's own household. You demonstrated Your power through 10 plagues. You parted the Red Sea. You delivered Your people.

And then at Sinai, You gave them the Law.

Not to save them. But to show them they couldn't save themselves.

"For no one will be justified in His sight by the works of the law, because the knowledge of sin comes through the law" (Romans 3:20).

The Law was a mirror showing us our need for a Savior. Every sacrifice pointed to THE Lamb. Every priest pointed to Christ the High Priest. Every command revealed we couldn't keep Your law on our own.

You continued to work for centuries through judges, through the tabernacle, through daily sacrifices. Always pointing to Christ. Always moving the plan forward.

Establishing the Royal Line Through David

When Your people asked for a king, they were rejecting You. You gave them what they wanted anyway and anointed Saul. When Saul failed, You chose David.

Through the Davidic Covenant, You promised that one of David's descendants would rule on the throne forever.

"When your time comes and you rest with your fathers, I will raise up after you your descendant, who will come from your body, and I will establish his kingdom. He is the one who will build a house for My name, and I will establish the throne of his kingdom forever" (2 Samuel 7:12-13).

The Redeemer would reign. Christ would be both Savior AND King.

You worked through David's victories over lions, bears, and giants. You worked through his failures — adultery, murder, and their consequences.

You preserved the royal line through Solomon, through the kingdom's division, through conquest and exile and return.

Setting the Stage Through Silence

By the time of Malachi, You'd given the prophets over 300 details about the coming Messiah. The plan was crystal clear.

He would be born in Bethlehem from David's line. Born of a virgin. A suffering servant who would be pierced for our rebellion. A conquering king who would reign forever. He would die for sins and rise again.

In this way, Christ would crush the serpent's head and restore fellowship with Your people who would walk with You forever.

Then 400 years of silence followed.

No prophets speaking Your inspired word. No recorded biblical miracles. No audible voice.

But You were still working. Building roads that would carry the gospel. Spreading Greek language that would unite the world for Scripture. Establishing Roman peace that would allow safe travel.

You used the silence to set the stage for Christ.

The Pattern of God's Work

When I study how You worked for thousands of years, I learn what persistence actually means.

You never waited for perfect conditions. Abraham wasn't morally perfect. The Israelites weren't ready. David wasn't sinless. You worked through imperfect people because perfect people don't exist. You work with what's available and require willing hearts, not flawless records.

You never quit when things didn't go Your way. Adam sinned. Humanity rebelled. Israel turned to idols. Kings failed. Prophets were rejected. But You didn't abandon the mission. You adjusted. You redirected. You kept going. Your plan was always Christ, and nothing could stop that.

You defined the end first, then worked backwards. Redemption was complete in Your mind before time began. But You worked through thousands of years of history to unfold it. Vision is instant. Fulfillment is

41

incremental. Just because something is planned doesn't mean it won't take time, sweat, and struggle to implement.

You never rushed. You took 4,000 years to prepare the world for Christ. Then You took 33 more years to prepare Christ to redeem the world. Patience isn't passive. It's powerful. It's working at the right pace to get the right result.

You worked through ordinary people and extraordinary power. Abraham the liar. Moses the murderer. David the adulterer. These weren't moral giants who earned the right to be part of Your plan. They were flawed humans who said yes when You called.

And You used extraordinary events. A global flood. Languages confused. An old lady giving birth. A sea parted. A giant slain.

You worked through the ordinary and the extraordinary. Through human failure and divine power. Through visible miracles and invisible faithfulness.

Ordinary People + Your Extraordinary Power + Time + Trials = Persistent Transformative Work

And You never quit.

Not when the entire world turned against You save Noah. Not when Your chosen people worshiped idols. Not when the kings You anointed fell into sin. Not when 400 years passed without a single prophet.

You kept Your eyes on the vision: faithful fellowship.

You kept working the plan: send Christ.

You kept Your promises. Every. Single. One.

What This Means for Me

My two-year 50 by 50 mission is nothing compared to Your 4,000-year redemption plan.

So when obstacles arise, remind me that You kept working even when every person on earth save one turned away from You.

When the odds are stacked against me, remind me that the same God who parted the Red Sea lives in me and fights for me.

When I want to quit at 80%, remind me that You kept moving forward for thousands of years to prepare the world for Christ.

When progress feels slow, remind me that You measure success in faithfulness and completion, not speed.

When people fail me, remind me that You worked through liars, murderers, and adulterers to accomplish Your plan.

When I'm tempted to start something new before finishing the old, remind me that You stayed focused on ONE mission for 4,000 years: send Christ.

Your patience becomes mine. Your persistence becomes mine. Your faithfulness becomes mine.

Not through trying harder. Through walking closer.

You PLANNED strategically — one Savior, one nation, the Law, the royal line, prophetic details.

You WORKED persistently — over thousands of years through imperfect humans and despite satanic opposition.

But the DO phase isn't complete until You cross the finish line.

Now show me the completion.

Because 4,000 years of preparation led to this moment: the arrival of Christ.

Show me how He FINISHED what You planned and started.

5

THE VICTORIOUS SAVIOR

DEAR FATHER,

For 4,000 years You worked toward one goal: redeem sinners and restore fellowship.

You DREAMED from Your character and desire.

You PLANNED and WORKED through people and obstacles.

And I'm with You through all of that. I love walking with You. I love dreaming big dreams. I love planning ways to bring those dreams to life. I love starting. I love working.

I avoid finishing.

But finishing is the climax of the DO phase. It's where planning and working reach their ultimate moment: victory.

You showed me this. Because You always see Your mission through to the end.

You don't just finish tasks. You CONQUER obstacles. You DEFEAT enemies. You TRIUMPH over impossibility.

So show me how Christ finished the work You gave Him to do.

The Prayerful Decision to Finish

In the Garden of Gethsemane, Jesus faced the choice every person must face: keep going or turn back.

In His humanity, He wanted to find another way. The physical torture He was about to endure was horrific — beating, mocking, crucifixion.

But worse than the physical pain was the spiritual darkness: bearing the weight of humanity's sin and experiencing Your wrath.

He had never sinned. He hates sin. Now He was about to become sin itself. To feel the separation from You that sin brings. To endure the darkness of Your judgment.

"Going a little farther, He fell facedown and prayed, 'My Father, if it is possible, let this cup pass from Me. Yet not as I will, but as You will'" (Matthew 26:39).

Three times He asked. Three times He surrendered.

"Yet not as I will, but as You will."

When the price of finishing was at its peak, Jesus turned to You. And made a prayerful decision. A choice. A deliberate act of obedience even when every human emotion was screaming for Him to stop.

Jesus didn't finish because it felt good. He finished because He CHOSE to.

He could have called angels to rescue Him. He could have struck everyone with blindness and escaped. He could have used the power of His words to destroy those who were about to destroy Him.

But He chose to finish instead.

Finishing requires surrender. It requires saying "Not my will, but Yours" when the final push demands everything you have.

Jesus made that choice. Then He allowed Himself to be arrested.

The Payment

They led Him to trial. False accusations. Physical beatings. Disrespectful mocking. He stood before the Sanhedrin and Pilate as a prisoner, enduring injustice without complaint.

"He was oppressed and afflicted, yet He did not open his mouth. Like a lamb led to the slaughter and like a sheep silent before her shearers, He did not open his mouth" (Isaiah 53:7).

Then they nailed Him to a cross.

His hands. His feet. A crown of thorns pressed into His skull. Crucified like a criminal between two thieves.

But the physical suffering wasn't the worst part.

At noon, darkness fell over the land and lasted for three hours. An unnatural darkness in the middle of the day.

"It was now about noon, and darkness came over the whole land until three, because the sun's light failed" (Luke 23:44-45a).

In those three dark hours, Jesus bore the weight of my sin. He took upon Himself the full punishment I deserved.

"He Himself bore our sins in His body on the tree, so that, having died to sins, we might live for righteousness. By His wounds you have been healed" (1 Peter 2:24).

I am healed because He experienced Your wrath and endured the separation and forsakenness that sin brings. That is a darkness no human soul could endure.

"He made the one who did not know sin to be sin for us, so that in Him we might become the righteousness of God" (2 Corinthians 5:21).

Friends gone. Flesh torn. Fellowship with You broken.

He could have quit in the middle of the darkness. He could have saved Himself from that agony.

But He endured it. For me.

Then, after experiencing Your full wrath, He gathered one final breath and declared in a loud voice: "It is finished" (John 19:30).

Not "I'm dying."

Not "It's over."

Not "I give up."

"It is FINISHED." A cry of victory!

Mission accomplished. Penalty of sin paid in full. Redemption completed. Victory secured.

All of human history — the 4,000 years of preparation — came to a climax in that one moment.

The sacrificial system? No longer needed.

The veil in the temple? Torn from top to bottom.

Access to You? RESTORED.

"Suddenly, the curtain of the sanctuary was torn in two from top to bottom, the earth quaked, and the rocks were split" (Matthew 27:51).

At the cross, Christ FINISHED the work of redemption by the shedding of His blood. His blood paid the price for my sin and restored access to You.

The task was complete. And death took hold.

The Proof

The world thought His *life* was done. Finished. Over. Complete.

After all, that conclusion made sense. He stopped breathing. His physical body died. They buried Him in a tomb.

Saturday, His body lay still in the grave.

But death has no power over the sinless. And Jesus is the only sinless One to ever live.

"Because we know that Christ, having been raised from the dead, will not die again. Death no longer rules over him" (Romans 6:9).

So on Sunday morning, You breathed new life into His earthly lungs. What a glorious victory over death when He came out of the tomb in His resurrected body!

"He is not here. For He has risen, just as He said" (Matthew 28:6a).

The resurrection wasn't just a miracle. It was VALIDATION.

You were declaring to all creation: "The sacrifice was ACCEPTED. The payment was SUFFICIENT. The work is COMPLETE."

Jesus was raised to life so I could be justified by a living Savior. His righteousness could not be applied to me if He stayed dead.

"He was delivered up for our trespasses and raised for our justification" (Romans 4:25).

The resurrection PROVED that Christ is who He said He is.

"Concerning his Son, Jesus Christ our Lord, who was a descendant of David according to the flesh and was appointed to be the powerful Son of God according to the Spirit of holiness by the resurrection of the dead" (Romans 1:4).

Finishing looks like VICTORY over the greatest enemy. Death tried to hold Him. Death FAILED.

The Triumph

I want to pause here to experience this victory. To feel what it's like to finish and WIN. Help me understand what Christ accomplished on that cross.

Sin's penalty? PAID IN FULL.

Not partially paid. Not mostly covered. Not "good enough for now."

Completely. Totally. Paid. Nothing left to pay for the wages of my sin. Only life to experience today and forevermore.

"But the gift of God is eternal life in Christ Jesus our Lord" (Romans 6:23b).

Your holy wrath? SATISFIED COMPLETELY.

You poured out every ounce of righteous anger I deserve for my rebellion on Christ. No part of Your wrath against me remains. All You see is Christ's blood when You look at me. My debt is ZERO.

"He Himself is the atoning sacrifice for our sins, and not only for ours, but also for those of the whole world" (1 John 2:2).

Satan's power? BROKEN FOREVER.

The prince of this world thought he won when Jesus died. But the resurrection CRUSHED his head just as You promised in Genesis 3:15.

"He disarmed the rulers and authorities and disgraced them publicly; He triumphed over them in Him" (Colossians 2:15).

Death's hold? DEFEATED UTTERLY.

Death tried to hold Jesus. Death FAILED. And because He lives, I will live too.

"Where, death, is your victory? Where, death, is your sting?" (1 Corinthians 15:55).

Separation from You? ENDED PERMANENTLY.

The veil was torn. The barrier is gone. I have ACCESS to You through Christ.

"For through Him we both have access in one Spirit to the Father" (Ephesians 2:18).

Fellowship with God? RESTORED ETERNALLY.

The dream You had before the foundation of the world — walking with people who are holy and blameless before You in love — is NOW POSSIBLE because of what Christ finished.

"Therefore, brothers and sisters, since we have boldness to enter the sanctuary through the blood of Jesus...let us draw near with a true heart in full assurance of faith, with our hearts sprinkled clean from an evil conscience and our bodies washed in pure water" (Hebrews 10:19, 22).

This is COMPLETION. This is VICTORY. This is what it looks like when the Faithful Finisher FINISHES.

Not just task completion. TRIUMPHANT CONQUEST.

What Comes After Completion

Jesus teaches me that finishing is costly. Decisive. Complete. Triumphant. And thorough.

Because Jesus didn't stop after the triumph. He took time to debrief His quest, rest after the resurrection, reap the rewards of a redeemed people, and take on a new role after His work of redemption was complete.

And that's where I've been fading. I cross finish lines (if I dare go that far) but skip what comes after. I complete the DO phase but abandon the REAP phase.

But I'm scared to go there. I'm scared to walk through that part of the process, so please show me why it's important. Help me understand why it matters.

Show me PHASE 3.

Show me what comes after completion.

Show me how finishing the work leads to finishing the TRANS-FORMATION and how the transformation leads to the capacity to take on the next mission.

6

THE CHARACTER TRANSFORMER

DEAR FATHER,

Finishing isn't just crossing the finish line. It's following through to the very end of the mission. It's completing PHASE 3: REAP.

The phase I've been skipping. The follow-through that completes the transformation.

To finish the work of redemption, Jesus prayed, surrendered, and followed through with Your plan. He knew exactly what was coming and chose to finish anyway.

The final push required Him to endure a spiritual, mental, emotional, and physical storm in order pay the price for my sin. Finishing demanded surrender. It demanded a decision.

Because finishing is where obedience costs the most.

This is why I fade at 80-90% (or sooner). Because the final stretch is where the battle is.

But Jesus didn't stop at the cross. He didn't declare "It is finished" and disappear.

He followed through the complete arc: Debrief, Rest, Reap Rewards.

That's what PHASE 3 looks like. And that's what I've been abandoning.

I know the outcome I want, but unlike You, my victory is not guaranteed.

In other words, I often don't get the results I anticipate. So I hold back to avoid disappointment. Or success.

If I don't promote my books, I can still believe they're valuable. If I don't share them, I don't have to face rejection.

But if I market them, they might not sell. Or they might sell and receive negative reviews. And then I'll be humiliated.

That fear-based vision keeps me writing — but not sharing.

The opposite outcome scares me, too.

If they *do* sell...

If people respond...

If money and visibility follow...

I fear placing my hope in success instead of You.

So sharing my work feels dangerous either way.

That's why the 50 by 50 Challenge forces me to think differently. *I know You've called me to this work. I know You've equipped me for it. I trust You to bless the obedience in a way that keeps me humble and generous.*

Still, I'm conflicted.

I'm afraid that if I finish all the way through, I'll receive only invisible rewards. That I'll grow in character but see no tangible fruit — no income, no impact, no changed lives.

Yet I don't want to chase tangible rewards, because I know the invisible ones matter more.

The tension lives right here.

I love the work. I love the process.

I struggle with the follow-through.

I've been afraid that finishing means losing purpose, that once the climax passes, the meaning drains away.

But faithful finishing doesn't stop at the climax. It completes the whole arc.

Finishing the whole arc creates *capacity*.

Just as Christ's finished work of redemption made room for the Spirit's work of sanctification, finishing opens space for what comes next.

So finishing isn't just crossing the line. It's completing the entire process.

PHASE 1: DREAM from character and desire.

PHASE 2: DO the work (plan, work, finish).

PHASE 3: REAP the transformation (debrief, rest, reap rewards).

Then DREAM AGAIN from new capacity.

But I can only dream from new capacity if I complete Phase 3. If I skip the REAP phase, there's no transformation. No new capacity. No higher floor to dream from next time.

That's the real purpose. Not achievement. Transformation.

When I finished the first marathon, I crossed the line and felt empty.

When I finished the 101 Day Challenge, I completed the tasks but not the transformation.

Because I skipped the final steps.

I thought finishing meant COMPLETION.

Now You're showing me it means *completion plus integration*.

The end goal is never the only goal. There is always an invisible mission behind the visible one.

That invisible mission is Christlikeness.

"For those He foreknew He also predestined to be conformed to the image of his Son, so that He would be the firstborn among many brothers and sisters" (Romans 8:29).

You want me to be like Christ.

You don't change through Your finished work — but the people You work through must. Otherwise faithful fellowship would be impossible.

That's why You care more about who I'm becoming than what I'm accomplishing.

The Invisible Mission

Every dream You give me has two finish lines.

The visible finish line is the deliverable: the book published, the race completed, the business launched.

The invisible finish line is the transformation: the faith deepened, the pride broken, the dependence strengthened.

You care about both.

You prospered Abraham, Joseph, Moses, David, Daniel — and You also weighed their hearts.

A wildly successful book written for self-glory is failure in Your economy.

A humble offering given for Your glory is eternal victory.

But here's what I've been missing. The invisible mission doesn't complete during the work. It completes *after* the work.

If I skip **DEBRIEF, REST, and REAP REWARDS**, the transformation stalls.

The task ends, but I stay the same.

That's why the final 10–20% is the hardest.

That's why You don't remove the pressure.

The struggle *is* the sanctification.

You weren't wasting time with Moses, Joseph, David, or Paul when You spent years testing and refining them before enabling them to accomplish their main mission. You were preparing them to survive success without being destroyed by it.

The tangible mission prepares the circumstances.

The invisible mission prepares *me*.

And PHASE 3 is where that preparation completes.

- PHASE 1: DREAM establishes the foundation (character/desire/vision).

- PHASE 2: DO executes the work (plan/work/finish the task).

- PHASE 3: REAP completes the transformation (debrief/rest/reap rewards).

Without Phase 3, I finish tasks but don't become someone new. I cross finish lines but don't claim the new identity. I accomplish goals but don't gain new capacity.

That's why this phase matters. Because the transformation You've been working in me throughout the DO phase doesn't happen AT the finish line. It happens AFTER.

Transformation Requires Death

Becoming like Christ doesn't just mean adding His qualities to my life. It means crucifying the parts of me that resist Him.

"I have been crucified with Christ, and I no longer live, but Christ lives in me. The life I now live in the body, I live by faith in the Son of God, who loved me and gave Himself for me" (Galatians 2:20).

Crucified.

This is the cost of transformation: my pride must die. My need for control must die. My self-reliance must die. My fear of the unknown must die. My comfort-seeking must die.

And death is painful.

This is why the finishing steps matter so much. Because it's in DEBRIEF, REST, and REAP REWARDS that I see what needs to die...and let You kill it.

When I debrief honestly: "Here's where my pride showed up. Here's where I tried to control instead of trust."

When I rest intentionally: "I'm letting go of the need to strive. I'm trusting You even when I'm not working."

When I reap rewards gratefully: "This transformation is Your work in me, not my achievement."

The old self dies. The new self emerges. Christlikeness increases.

The Spirit's Daily Work

Justification happened in a moment. The moment I believed, I was declared righteous. My eternal destiny is secure. I am forgiven, adopted, sealed.

But sanctification is progressive. It's the lifelong process of becoming in practice (like Christ) what I already am in position (Your daughter).

"Therefore, my dear friends, just as you have always obeyed, so now, not only in my presence but even more in my absence, work out your own salvation with fear and trembling. For it is God who is working in you both to will and to work according to His good purpose" (Philippians 2:12-13).

The Spirit is working in me every day. During WORK, He empowers me to do what I can't do on my own. During DEBRIEF, He reveals what I need to see. During REST, He lets transformation settle. During REAP REWARDS, He solidifies my new identity and showers me with blessings that are tangible fruit from my labor (although I don't always see this fruit right away).

This happens in every cycle. Every dream I pursue. Every project I finish.

Each round through PHASE 3 transforms me a little more.

It's not instant. It's daily. Progressive. Cumulative.

But it's certain. Because You always finish what You start.

"I am sure of this, that He who started a good work in you will carry it on to completion until the day of Christ Jesus" (Philippians 1:6).

So teach me to complete PHASE 3. All three steps: Debrief, Rest. Reap Rewards.

Debrief

On the same day that Jesus rose from the grave, He walked with two confused disciples on the road to Emmaus who were discussing "the things concerning Jesus of Nazareth" (Luke 24:19a).

They were having trouble making sense of the death of Jesus. They thought He had come to set up His kingdom. They misunderstood the mission of redemption. So He reminded them of the story.

"Then beginning with Moses and all the Prophets, He interpreted for them the things concerning Himself in all the Scriptures" (Luke 24:27).

The purpose of a debrief, then, is to review what happened, extract wisdom, and clarify meaning while it's fresh.

In other words, Jesus started the debrief by evaluating the measurable actions, then dug to extract the invisible fruit. He didn't need to review His work to understand the wisdom and meaning behind it all, but the disciples needed help making sense of everything.

Jesus didn't need the debrief. They did.

And then He rested.

Rest

Rest means intentional recovery before the next thing.

Not passive laziness. Active, purposeful stepping away from work to recover and prepare for the next level work.

In His resurrected body, Jesus made Himself known to the women who came to the tomb, then to His disciples, then to over 500 people who witnessed Him alive and well.

He celebrated His resurrected life for 40 days after His great victory. Then He ascended to heaven and sat down at Your right hand.

"After making purification for sins, He sat down at the right hand of the Majesty on high" (Hebrews 1:3b).

Earthly priests stood because the work was never complete. Jesus sat because His work was done.

"Every priest stands day after day ministering and offering the same sacrifices time after time, which can never take away sins. But this man, after offering one sacrifice for sins forever, sat down at the right hand of God" (Hebrews 10:11-12).

Since Christ is my sinless Savior, His sacrifice was the ONLY sacrifice needed to pay the debt of my sin.

One sacrifice. Forever. Done.

Sitting doesn't mean resting from all work. It means the sacrifice is DONE, but the mission to enjoy faithful fellowship with a holy and blameless people continues.

That's why Jesus intercedes for me now.

"Therefore, He is able to save completely those who come to God through Him, since He always lives to intercede for them" (Hebrews 7:25).

Jesus stands before You and pleads my case when I stumble. He reminds You that my debt is paid, that I am covered by His blood, that I belong to You as Your child.

"Who is the one who condemns? Christ Jesus is the one who died, but even more, has been raised; He also is at the right hand of God and intercedes for us" (Romans 8:34).

He never stops advocating for me. He always lives to intercede.

Jesus followed through to the very end and completed the entire earthly arc necessary for my salvation: virgin birth → sinless life → sacrificial death → burial → resurrection → celebration → ascension.

Through Christ, You show me that true finishing includes follow-through after the task is done.

You also show me through Christ that finishing creates capacity. He finished His job of redemption so the Holy Spirit could come and live in my heart to do His job of sanctification.

So completion isn't the death of purpose like I once feared; it's the birth of new possibility in that it creates capacity for what's next.

Reap Rewards

Christ is still reaping the rewards of redemption.

The fruit of His work is *me*. Redeemed. Restored. Welcomed into fellowship. Part of the family. Forever.

Everyone who confesses Christ as Savior and walks with God as a result is the fruit of the Your love and Christ's sacrifice.

And we get to come boldly before Your throne because of Christ:

"Therefore, let us approach the throne of grace with boldness, so that we may receive mercy and find grace to help us in time of need" (Hebrews 4:16).

You didn't send Christ to live and die and live again so He could reap external prizes. He came to reap the reward of eternal souls.

The immediate rewards You prepare for me aren't about external prizes, either. It's about harvesting what the work produces in me.

"Let us not get tired of doing good, for we will reap at the proper time if we don't give up" (Galatians 6:9).

For me, the rewards aren't just revenue from book sales or medals at the end of a finished race. The rewards are who I become through the process.

Deeper faith. Stronger discipline. Greater capacity. Renewed mind. Transformed character.

Reaping rewards means celebrating this transformation and declaring: "I am different now. I am not who I was when I started. I have become someone new."

Without reaping rewards, I can't solidify the new identity. I finish the task but stay the old version of myself.

These three steps work together:

DEBRIEF extracts the wisdom: "Here's what I learned. Here's who I became."

REST lets it settle: "I'm giving this time to take root in me."

REAP REWARDS seals the identity: "I am different now. I am this new person capable of stewarding tangible results for the glory of God."

This is PHASE 3: REAP. The follow-through that completes the transformation.

Complete all three, and I finish the ENTIRE cycle. Not just the task. The TRANSFORMATION.

Then I'm ready to DREAM AGAIN. But now I dream from a new level. Because I'm someone new with new capacity.

PHASE 1 → PHASE 2 → PHASE 3 → PHASE 1 (from higher ground)

Each completion raises my floor. Each summit becomes my new base camp.

This is the 3-Phase Follow Through: DREAM → DO → REAP → DREAM AGAIN.

And each round makes me more like Christ.

The Complete Cycle

I understand the 3-Phase Follow Through now:

DREAM: Character → Driving Desire → Dream →
DO: Plan → Work → Finish →
REAP: Debrief → Rest → Reap Rewards →

Then DREAM AGAIN from new capacity as a transformed person.

The 3-Phase Follow Through is a cycle, but not an endless, repetitive, pointless circle. Because each completion creates capacity. Each round strengthens the foundation, enabling me to build bigger and climb higher.

Father, this is how You finish — except for the fact that You don't transform or increase Your capacity. You don't need to. You are already perfect. But You model these steps for me because I always have room for improvement. I always have a next level to aspire to reach.

But knowing the process isn't enough. I need to LIVE it.

Show me what this looks like in my daily life. Show me how to apply this to the 50 by 50 mission. Show me how to become a faithful finisher who walks with You through every step of the cycle.

Show me how to live a well-done life.

7

— · —

LIVING A WELL DONE LIFE

DEAR FATHER,

I came to this conversation as a fader.

I'm leaving as a finisher.

Not because I've finished the 50 by 50 Challenge. Not because I've proven myself capable. Not because I've mastered the complete finishing cycle.

But because I've walked with You through these pages. And walking with You transforms me.

I now know what to put off: the fear that success will pull me from You. The belief that dreams don't matter. The identity as someone who fades at 80%. The lie that finishing means losing purpose. The skipping the final steps that keeps me starting but never completing.

I now know what to put on: certainty rooted in Your character. Belief that dreams are portals of transformation. Identity as a finisher made in Your image. The truth that finishing creates capacity. The confidence that comes from walking with You.

"You took off your former way of life, the old self that is corrupted by deceitful desires, you are being renewed in the spirit of your minds, and you put on the new self, the one created according to God's likeness in righteousness and purity of the truth" (Ephesians 4:22-24).

I now know how to renew my mind: immerse myself in the truth of who You are daily. Show up for focused work. Walk with You through the entire finishing cycle. Trust Your character instead of my willpower. Enjoy faithful fellowship more than visible outcomes.

"Now faith is the reality of what is hoped for, the proof of what is not seen" (Hebrews 11:1).

I don't have to wait until I've published 50 books to BE a finisher. Faith IS the substance. Your character IS the evidence.

I am no longer a fader. I am a finisher like You.

Not because I've proven it yet. But because "without faith it is impossible to please God, since the one who draws near to Him must believe that He exists and that He rewards those who seek Him" (Hebrews 11:6).

I believe You exist. I believe You are the Faithful Finisher. I believe You're forming me into Your image. And I believe You reward those who diligently seek You.

So I walk with certainty in who I am because of who You are.

The transformation isn't waiting at the finish line. The transformation is happening right now as I walk with You every day.

Now teach me to walk through all three phases. Not just once, but as a way of life.

Show me how to DREAM with You. Show me how to DO what I dream with You. Show me how to follow all the way through so that I can REAP what You provide.

And show me how each completion raises my floor so I can dream again from new capacity.

PHASE 1: Dreaming With You

Please help me align my CHARACTER, DESIRES, and DREAMS with Yours.

I used to dream without examining where those dreams came from. I'd get excited about big goals without asking: "Does this align with who You designed me to be? Is this about proving something or pursuing You?"

Now I know dreams that don't flow from my God-designed character and my desire for faithful fellowship with You will always leave me empty even if I achieve them.

CHARACTER

Teach me to start here. Who did You design me to be? What are my God-given strengths? What lights me up because it aligns with how You made me?

Help me see myself the way You see me — not through the world's definition of success or comparison to others, but through the unique design You built into me before I was born.

Show me the gifts You've given, the passions You've planted, the experiences You've allowed. All of it shapes who I am. All of it points to what I'm made for.

Don't let me chase dreams that require me to be someone I'm not. Don't let me waste energy trying to copy someone else's calling. Root me in who YOU made ME to be.

DRIVING DESIRE

Then help me examine my desires. Do I want this because it will draw me closer to You? Or because I think it will make me significant, successful, impressive?

Am I using this dream to fill needs only You can satisfy — acceptance, worth, belonging, purpose?

Or am I dreaming from a place of wanting faithful fellowship with You, knowing that walking with You is the reward, and everything else is just the adventure You're inviting me into?

Help me vet my desires against Yours constantly. Sin is still present in me. Satan is still at work trying to drive me away from You. So check my motives daily.

When I discover desires rooted in pride, performance, or people-pleasing, uproot them. Replace them with desires that flow from Your character and align with Your mission to redeem and restore mankind.

DREAM

Only then should I form the DREAM. The specific target. The tangible goal.

Not a vague wish like "get healthier" or "write more." But a concrete, measurable dream: "Run a 10k a month" or "Publish a book by my birthday."

Help me dream boldly when my character and desires are aligned with You. Help me dream with clarity, specificity, and faith.

And when dreams emerge from godly character and God-aligned desires, give me courage to pursue them without fear of pride or failure. Because dreams rooted in You won't pull me from You. They'll draw me closer.

"Commit your activities to the Lord, and your plans will be established" (Proverbs 16:3).

PHASE 2: Doing with You

Help me execute the DO phase: PLAN, WORK, and FINISH like You.

PLAN

Teach me to PLAN like You.

When I have a God-aligned dream, show me what the end looks like. Let me see it clearly. Then help me work backwards: what needs to happen right before the end? And before that? And before that?

You revealed Your plan little by little. You didn't overwhelm us with the entire roadmap at once. You gave just enough light for the next step. So help me to trust You rather than overplan or attempt to figure out every detail before taking action.

I don't need to see the entire path to all 50 books. I just need to see the plan for the next one. Then the one after that. Little by little progress.

Help me break my mission into phases the way You did with redemption. Each book series becomes a phase. Each phase serves the overall mission but has its own strategic focus.

And Father, help me surrender my plans to You regularly. You redirect obedient people. As long as my motives are grounded in desiring faithful fellowship with You, I can pursue my dreams with relentless determination and trust You to redirect me if I get off track.

WORK

Help me WORK like You.

You showed up consistently day after day for thousands of years. When I don't see or feel You working doesn't mean You've quit or abandoned me. It means You're doing what needs to be done to set up the next phase.

Help me show up consistently. Even when I don't feel like it. Even when the work is hard. Even when I can't see progress or tangible rewards. I simply need to show up and do the work You've called me to do.

Help me work through obstacles. Not avoid them. Not wait for perfect conditions. But expect and welcome them because obstacles keep me connected to You. The greater the obstacle, the more I get to depend on You and let You show Yourself strong through me.

Help me work progressively, step by step, little by little. Small daily actions compound over time. 50 focused minutes today might not feel like much, but 50 minutes every day for two years? That's transformational.

FINISH

And Father, help me FINISH what I start. Not just get to 80% and move on to something new. But push through to COMPLETION. Cross the finish line. Declare "It is finished" over each project.

Because completion matters to You. And what matters to You must matter to me.

"Whatever you do, do it from the heart, as something done for the Lord and not for people" (Colossians 3:23).

PHASE 3: Reaping With You

Teach me to complete the REAP phase: DEBRIEF, REST, and REAP REWARDS.

DEBRIEF

Show me how to DEBRIEF effectively.

I've been skipping this step far too often. I finish the task, then immediately move on without extracting the wisdom, without identifying who I became, without seeing the transformation.

No more.

Help me debrief daily. At the end of each day, let me pause and ask: "What did I learn about God today? Who am I becoming? What needs to change tomorrow?"

Help me debrief weekly. Every week, let me review: " What adventures did I experience? What worked? What didn't? What patterns am I seeing? What adjustments do I need to make?"

And help me debrief after every completed project. When I finish a book, remind me to ask: "Who was I before I started this? Who am I now that I've finished? What fruit did this produce in me? What did I learn? How can I share this with people who need the transformation this book provides?"

This is collaborative reflection WITH You. Assess my loyalty. My faithfulness. The quality of my effort. Help me extract the wisdom so I don't repeat the same mistakes and so I can celebrate growth I might not see on my own.

"Search me, God, and know my heart; test me and know my concerns. See if there is any offensive way in me; lead me in the everlasting way" (Psalm 139:23-24).

Without debrief, I can't access the transformation. The lessons remain buried. The growth stays invisible. I accomplish the task but miss the becoming.

So Father, make this a non-negotiable rhythm in my life. Debrief WITH You. Daily. Weekly. After every project. That way I extract the wisdom while it's fresh so I can grow closer to You and become more like Christ.

REST

Father, remind me to REST.

But You modeled rest in creation. Day 7. Intentional recovery after six days of focused work. You weren't tired. You rested to establish a pattern for me.

Help me rest weekly. One day where I step away from work to let my brain take a break. One day to trust You in the quiet.

Help me rest between projects. When I finish a book, let me take time off before starting the next one. Let me read. Play. Do things that are active and fun and adventurous.

And Father, help me say no to new opportunities until rest is complete. The urge to start something new before recovering from the last thing is strong. It feels exciting. Productive. But it's sabotage.

"Come to me, all of you who are weary and burdened, and I will give you rest" (Matthew 11:28).

Rest creates space between effort and reward. It prevents burnout and the premature starting of the next thing.

Without rest, I lose my passion. I fade.

So Father, teach me to rest with intention. Not sporadic, aimless activity. Not guilty, anxious downtime. But confident, purposeful recovery that trusts You're still with me even when I'm not working.

REAP REWARDS

Help me REAP THE REWARDS You've given through each finished work.

I've been refusing to celebrate. Refusing to acknowledge victories. Refusing to receive the rewards because I'm afraid celebration will fuel pride or make me think I've "arrived."

But rewards aren't just external achievements. The rewards are WHO I BECOME through the process.

So help me reap those rewards. Help me celebrate each book published — not because I'm amazing, but because You're faithful and You worked through me to accomplish it.

Help me identify the transformation. Receive the fruit. Steward whatever revenue You provide. Serve the readers you bring into my world by training them to chase their own dreams.

The rewards are there. The fruit is ready for harvest. But if I don't reap it, it rots on the vine.

So Father, break my resistance to celebration. My refusal to receive rewards. My fear that acknowledging growth means I'm proud.

Without reaping rewards, I accomplish things but never become someone new. I cross finish lines but stay the same person.

So help me complete the process. Debrief. Rest. Reap rewards. THEN dream again from my new level.

The Perpetual Ascent

Father, I see it now.

Each completion raises my floor. Each harvest increases my capacity. Each summit becomes my new base camp.

I'm not climbing to arrive. I'm climbing to ascend.

Round 1: SMALL Capacity → Dream → Do → Reap → MEDIUM Capacity

Round 2: MEDIUM Capacity → Bolder Dream → Harder Do → Bigger Reap → GREATER Capacity

Round 3: GREATER Capacity → Crazier Dream → Tougher Do → Greater Reap → EXPANDED Capacity

The dream gets bolder. The work gets tougher. The harvest gets bigger.

But I never cap out. Because You never stop transforming me.

Each round through the 3-Phase Follow Through makes me more like Christ:

- More dependent on You as I DREAM.

- More obedient to You as I DO the work my dreams require.

- More transformed into the image of Christ as I REAP the harvest You produce through me.

And each transformation creates capacity for the next assignment.

Yesterday's impossible becomes today's achievable. Today's summit becomes tomorrow's starting line.

This is what it means to live a well-done life: walking with You through every phase, completing every cycle, becoming more like Christ with each ascent.

So keep me climbing, Father. Keep me faithful. Keep me finishing.

Because I'm not doing this for achievement. I'm doing this for fellowship with You — to know You deeply, to become like Christ, to experience Your power, to bring You glory, and to serve You eternally.

That's how I live a well done life.

CLOSING PRAYER

Dear Father,

You are the Faithful Finisher.

You planned redemption before the foundation of the world. You worked for 4,000 years through ordinary people and extraordinary power. You finished the work of salvation through Christ on the cross. And You're still working today, transforming me from the inside out.

You never quit. You never abandon what You start. You always see Your mission through to completion.

And You've shown me that finishing isn't crossing the finish line. It's completing the entire 3-Phase Follow Through:

DREAM: Character → Driving Desire → Dream →

DO: Plan → Work → Finish →

REAP: Debrief → Rest → Reap Rewards →

Then DREAM AGAIN from new capacity.

You've taught me that the invisible mission (Christlikeness) always matters more than the tangible mission (the books, the races, the impact).

You've revealed that my certainty doesn't come from my willpower but from Your character.

And You've transformed me.

I Am No Longer a Fader

I am a finisher.

Not because I've proven it with 50 books or 50 runs or 50 transformed lives.

But because I walk with the God who finishes.

Your character is my certainty. Your faithfulness is my foundation. Your promises are my proof.

"Therefore, if anyone is in Christ, he is a new creation; the old has passed away, and see, the new has come!" (2 Corinthians 5:17).

I am a new creation. The old has passed away. The new has come.

The fader is crucified. The finisher is raised.

I am who You say I am. I can do what You empower me to do. I will finish what You've called me to finish.

Not in my strength, but in Yours.

Not for my glory, but for Yours.

Not by my willpower, but through faithful fellowship with You.

The 50 by 50 Mission

Victory doesn't mean hitting all three targets perfectly: 50 books, 50 10Ks, 50 transformed lives. I'm aiming for those targets because I need tangible targets to pursue to keep me climbing on track. But victory means moving forward with focus and fire, doing the work You've called me to do while relying on You.

As long as I'm walking with You through the complete 3-Phase Follow Through — DREAM through REAP — I win.

Here are the lifestyle conditions I'm setting to keep myself aligned:

First condition: Love You and love my neighbors.

"Love the Lord your God with all your heart, with all your soul, and with all your mind. This is the greatest and most important command. The second is like it: Love your neighbor as yourself" (Matthew 22:37-39).

Loving You with all of me ensures my heart stays humble, aligned, and loyal. Loving my neighbors keeps me service-minded and others-focused. This is the CHARACTER foundation that drives everything else.

Second condition: Move my body at least a mile every day.

Run, walk, bike, or hike at least a mile a day, no matter what, unless circumstances are beyond my control. This keeps me physically disciplined while I race forward creatively. It's a daily reminder that finishing requires both spiritual and physical endurance.

Third condition: 50 focused minutes of work six days a week.

Show up for 50 focused minutes every day except one. Actual work — drafting, editing, publishing, marketing. This is the work that moves books from concept to completion and gets the books in front of people who need them.

On the seventh day, I use those 50 minutes to DEBRIEF the week, REST intentionally, and REAP REWARDS by celebrating progress and planning the next week.

Because transformation doesn't happen in one heroic push. It happens in daily faithfulness compounded over time.

You'll provide the inspiration. You'll open the doors. You'll bring the fruit.

I just have to show up and work with a humble heart that is on fire for You. That's how I slay any giant that dares stand in my way.

My Prayer for Ongoing Transformation

So transform me into a faithful finisher who expects great things from You and always finds a way to do what I dream when I stick to You and my strengths.

Make me more like Christ. Take my life and show Yourself great through me. Let me start strong, stay strong, and finish stronger.

Help me complete the entire 3-Phase Follow Through every time:

PHASE 1 - DREAM

Help me dream from godly character that aligns with Your desire for fellowship. Keep my motives pure. Guard my heart from pride and selfishness.

PHASE 2 - DO

Help me plan strategically, work persistently, and finish faithfully. When obstacles arise, remind me You work through them, not around them. When I want to quit at 80%, remind me You kept moving forward for thousands of years.

PHASE 3 - REAP

Help me debrief with honesty, rest with intention, and reap rewards with gratitude. Break my resistance to celebration. Teach me to claim the new identity You've forged in me through the process.

Then help me DREAM AGAIN from my new capacity.

Because finishing compounds. Every struggle conquered becomes strength gained. Each finish prepares me for what comes next.

Keep Me Anchored

Remind me always that You love me, walk with me, and equip me to fulfill bold dreams aligned with Your desires so that I enjoy the process of becoming like Christ and leading others to You, all for the praise of Your glory.

When obstacles arise, remind me that You kept working even when every person on earth save one turned away from You.

When the odds are stacked against me, remind me that the same God who parted the Red Sea lives in me and fights for me.

When I want to quit at 80%, remind me that You kept moving forward for thousands of years to prepare the world for Christ.

When progress feels slow, remind me that You measure success in faithfulness and completion, not speed.

When people fail me, remind me that You worked through liars, murderers, and adulterers to accomplish Your plan.

When I'm tempted to start something new before finishing the old, remind me that You stayed focused on ONE mission for 4,000 years: send Christ.

Your patience becomes mine. Your persistence becomes mine. Your faithfulness becomes mine.

Not through trying harder. Through walking closer.

I am a finisher because You are the Faithful Finisher.

And I am Yours.

In Christ,
Amen

YOUR TURN TO FINISH

Dear Reader,

You just walked through the greatest project ever completed: God's 4,000-year quest to redeem mankind, and His 2,000+ year (and still going) quest to restore fellowship post-redemption.

You saw His vision, His strategy, His persistent work, His victorious completion, and the transformation it created.

But here's what I realized as I finished writing this book: God turned the plan of redemption into a STORY.

Redemption wasn't a task on His divine to-do list. It was an epic adventure with prophecies and fulfillment, heroes and villains, preparation and climax, suffering and triumph. It was an adventure that revealed who He is through what He did.

And He's still writing that story through your life.

Your life isn't a collection of projects to manage. It's an adventure to be lived. Because it's part of the story God is writing through You to fulfill His mission to redeem and restore mankind.

Every trial is character development. Every struggle is rising action. Every victory points back to Him. Every transformation reveals more of His nature. You're not here to be productive. **You're here to be a faithful servant in a story that brings God glory.**

When you're managing projects, it's hard to see how every piece of your life works together to tell His story. When you're living an adventure, finishing feels like purposeful fun.

So the question isn't "How do I finish more projects?" The question is: "What story is God writing through my life right now?"

To identify that story, you first need to figure out where you fade in the process: DREAM, DO, OR REAP.

Where Do You Fade?

The 3-Phase Follow Through is a cycle, but not an endless loop. You're not repeating the same level forever. Because yesterday's impossible becomes today's achievable.

You may not fade at the same place every time. I don't. But you probably have a pattern. A consistent phase where momentum dies and projects stall.

Read through these statements and give yourself a score of 1-5 for each.

1 = Never true for me

2 = Rarely true

3 = Sometimes true

4 = Often true

5 = Always true for me

At the end of each phase, tally your score to determine your Adventurer type.

THE STARTING LINE: DREAM PHASE
(Character – Driving Desire – Dreams)

- _____ I'm not sure what I'm naturally good at or how God designed me.

- _____ I feel guilty when I want things for myself.

- _____ I have vague goals like "get healthy" but no specific targets.

- _____ I don't believe my dreams matter to God.

- _____ I start lots of projects/ideas but never commit to ONE.

- _____ I'm surviving day-to-day but not really pursuing anything.

TOTAL: _____ / 30

THE MIDDLE MILES: DO PHASE
(Plan – Work – Finish)

- _____ I plan extensively but rarely execute.

- _____ I start strong but quit when projects get hard (around 80%).

- _____ I'm constantly missing deadlines.

- _____ I abandon projects right before finishing.

- _____ I sabotage myself when success is within reach.

- _____ I leave a trail of almost-finished projects behind me.

TOTAL: _____ / 30

THE FINISH LINE & BEYOND: REAP PHASE
(Debrief – Rest – Reap Rewards)

- _____ I finish things but don't stop to learn from them.

- _____ I move on immediately without celebrating victories.

- _____ I finish projects but feel empty afterward.

- _____ I equate rest with laziness.

- _____ I can't receive praise or acknowledge growth.

- _____ I accomplish things but wonder "Is this all there is?"

TOTAL: _____ / 30

Now identify YOUR pattern: Where do you consistently fade? Which phase was your highest score?

- **Highest score at the Starting Line:** You're a **DORMANT WARRIOR**
  Fade point: CHARACTER, DRIVING DESIRE, or DREAMS (Steps 1-3)

- **Highest score in the Middle Miles:** You're a **HESITANT HERO**
  Fade point: PLANS, WORK, or FINISH (Steps 4-6)

- **Highest score at the Finish Line & Beyond:** You're an **EMPTY CONQUEROR**
  Fade point: DEBRIEF, REST, or REAP REWARDS (Steps 7-9)

That's where the battle is. That's where you need to focus your energy. That's where God wants to transform you. And if you scored high in each phase, no worries. Just pick ONE to focus on improving first.

Three Types of Adventurers

As you think about where you fade, you likely recognize yourself in one of three adventure archetypes:

The Dormant Warrior

You're surviving, not thriving. Work, family, sleep, repeat. You move through life on autopilot with no sense of where you're going or who you're becoming.

You're not pursuing adventures because you've never let yourself dream. Or you've given up on dreaming because it feels selfish, impractical, or impossible.

But God created you to live an epic adventure for His glory, not just exist in the shadows.

"For we are His workmanship, created in Christ Jesus for good works, which God prepared ahead of time for us to do" (Ephesians 2:10).

He designed you with unique strengths, passions, and purpose. He prepared specific missions for you before you were born. Adventures that will transform you into someone capable of deeper fellowship with Him and shine for the praise of His glory.

The issue isn't that you can't dream. It's that you don't believe your dreams matter. You've accepted the lie that survival is enough.

It's not.

God didn't work out the plan of redemption for 4,000 years and invest over 2,000 more years sanctifying His people just so you could coast through life burying your dreams. He's inviting you into His mission to redeem and restore mankind. Your role in that mission is your adventure.

Your adventure could be working your ordinary job or being an ordinary parent or living an ordinary life. Great! Be the best ordinary *you* you can be. And keep getting better at being you. Do that by setting targets to keep improving in whatever mission God called you to. And enjoy the journey along the way.

When you do ordinary things well to the glory of God, you become extraordinary in God's eyes.

Where you fade: PHASE 1: DREAM

What you need: Permission to dream and clarity about who God designed you to be. Seek that permission from God (He'll grant it!) and ask for the clarity you need (He'll answer you!).

The Hesitant Hero

You hear the call. You have dreams. You might even have plans. But fear keeps you paralyzed at the threshold.

You start lots of projects with genuine excitement. But somewhere around 80%, you fade. You abandon quests just before the breakthrough. You leave a trail of almost-finished adventures behind you.

Maybe you fear that finishing will pull you away from God. Maybe you believe your dreams don't really matter. Maybe you've convinced yourself that staying small protects you from pride or disappointment.

David faced Goliath not because he was the strongest warrior but because he knew the God who fights for him. "The Lord who rescued me from the paw of the lion and the paw of the bear will rescue me from the hand of this Philistine" (1 Samuel 17:37).

Your adventure is waiting. The call is real. Will you answer it?

Where you fade: PHASE 2: DO

What you need: Courage to take action and push through the final 20% when faith costs the most. Rely on God, and He will see you through any challenge.

"Haven't I commanded you: be strong and courageous? Do not be afraid or discouraged, for the Lord your God is with you wherever you go" (Joshua 1:9).

The Empty Conqueror

You're productive. Disciplined. You cross finish lines, hit goals, complete what you start. But at the end of every victory, there's no joy. No celebration. Just a hollow "What now?"

You finish, but you don't feel fulfilled. You wonder if you're chasing the wrong dreams. You suspect there's supposed to be more than checking boxes and moving to the next quest.

You might be finishing adventures the world told you to pursue instead of the ones God designed you for. Or worse, you're finishing for your glory instead of His.

But there's another possibility: Your dreams ARE aligned. You're doing the work God called you to. You're following through faithfully. But you're not completing PHASE 3. You skip the debrief, rush past the rest, and refuse the rewards.

But when it's time to receive the rewards — the wisdom, the rest, the transformation, the fruit, the blessing — you can't let yourself have them.

You're afraid receiving will make you proud. You don't feel worthy of celebration. You're uncomfortable with being seen or blessed. Deep down, you don't trust that God's generosity is safe. In short, You don't trust that God is a REWARDER of those who seek Him.

So you finish, but you refuse the reward. You complete the work, but you won't let yourself become someone new.

"For am I now trying to persuade people, or God? Or am I striving to please people? If I were still trying to please people, I would not be a servant of Christ" (Galatians 1:10).

The solution isn't to stop finishing. It's to **realign your heart, complete the transformation, and learn to receive.**

"And my God will supply all your needs according to His riches in glory in Christ Jesus" (Philippians 4:19).

First, return to PHASE 1. Are your dreams rooted in God's character and your desire for fellowship with Him? Or are you chasing success to prove yourself, earn validation, or fill needs only God can satisfy? When you DREAM from fellowship instead of performance, finishing feels purposeful.

Then, complete PHASE 3 — all the way through.

Don't skip the debrief. You finish and immediately move to the next thing because reflection feels unproductive. But without extracting the wisdom, you can't access the transformation. Stop. Ask God: What did I learn? Who did I become? Let Him show you the fruit before you move on.

Don't skip the rest. You equate rest with laziness. You're afraid stopping will kill your momentum. But rest isn't wasted time — it's biblically necessary for spiritual, physical, mental, and emotional health. Trust that God is still with you when you're not working. Let yourself recover before the next thing.

Don't refuse the rewards. Let yourself receive what God wants to give. The transformation. The fruit. The visible blessing. Trust that God doesn't give blessing before He's prepared you to steward it. He transforms you THROUGH the work so you can receive the rewards WITH humility. Trust that you can steward success humbly when you're walking closely with the God who gives it.

When you finish for God's glory and complete all of PHASE 3 with God-aligned dreams, the emptiness disappears. You discover the reward isn't just at the finish line. It's in the walking WITH Him and becoming a more capable child of God.

Where you fade: PHASE 1 (misaligned dreams) and/or PHASE 3 (skipping debrief, rest, or refusing rewards)

What you need: Realign your dreams with God's design. Then follow all the way through — debrief honestly, rest intentionally, and receive gratefully. When finishing flows from fellowship and you complete the entire transformation, fulfillment follows.

How to Live Your Adventure

Wherever you are — struggling with the start, hesitating at the threshold, or finishing but empty — here's how to become a faithful finisher:

STEP 1: Identify Your Fade Phase

Take the quiz above. Be honest about your pattern. Which phase do you consistently abandon?

- **PHASE 1: DREAM?** You struggle with character clarity, believing dreams matter, or setting specific targets.

- **PHASE 2: DO?** You plan but don't execute, or you start strong but quit at 80%, or you sabotage right before the finish line.

- **PHASE 3: REAP?** You finish tasks but skip the debrief, rest, and celebration that complete the transformation.

That's your battle. That's where God wants to transform you. That's where you need to focus your energy.

Don't try to fix everything at once. Just identify the ONE phase where you typically fade.

STEP 2: Choose One Quest to Practice All 3 Phases

Pick one project. One dream. One adventure where you'll intentionally practice the complete 3-Phase Follow Through.

Not your biggest dream. Not your scariest goal. Pick something achievable but meaningful. Something that matters enough to push you but won't overwhelm you.

This is your test case. Your training ground. Your opportunity walk through all three phases with God to learn faithful finishing.

PHASE 1: DREAM

- **CHARACTER:** Who did God design you to be? What are your God-given strengths?

- **DRIVING DESIRE:** Are you grounding your desire in God's desire for fellowship? Or are you chasing achievement to fill needs only God can satisfy?

- **DREAM:** What's the specific, concrete target? Not "get healthier" but "run a 10K by June 15th."

PHASE 2: DO

- **PLAN:** What are the strategic steps? Break it into phases. Little by little progress. Surrender the plan to God regularly.

- **WORK:** Show up daily even when you don't feel like it. Work through obstacles, not around them. Expect trials and welcome them as opportunities to depend on God.

- **FINISH:** Cross the finish line. Declare "It is finished" over this project. Don't stop at 99%.

PHASE 3: REAP

- **DEBRIEF:** What did you learn? Who did you become? What worked? What didn't? Extract the wisdom while it's fresh.

- **REST:** Take intentional recovery time before the next thing. Weekly sabbath. Between-project breaks. Let your body, soul, heart, and mind take a break.

- **REAP REWARDS:** Celebrate the victory. Identify the transformation. Receive the fruit. Solidify your new identity.

Then **DREAM AGAIN** from your new level.

STEP 3: Expect Resistance and Walk With Others

You identified where you typically fade in Step 1. That's where the battle will be fierce.

If you fade in the **DREAM** phase, expect guilt when you let yourself want something. Expect doubt that your dreams matter. Prepare for it. Pray through it. Push through it.

If you fade in the **DO** phase, expect to want to quit in the messy middle. Expect fear when success is within reach. Resist it. Remember who fights for you. Keep going.

If you fade in **REAP** phase, expect to feel the urge to move on without reflection. Expect guilt when you rest. Silence that voice. Debrief is obedience. Rest is obedience. Celebration is worship.

The enemy doesn't want you to become a faithful finisher because faithful finishers are dangerous to his mission to keep you separated from God. Finishers accomplish what God calls them to do in God's strength.

So when you hit YOUR fade phase, remember: that's exactly where transformation happens.

And don't do it alone.

You can finish with God alone because God is the only One you need. But He designed us for relationship. So working WITH OTHER PEOPLE makes the mission more achievable and keeps you faithful when you would otherwise quit on your own.

God worked through PEOPLE for 4,000 years. Abraham, Moses, David — none of them accomplished the mission solo. They needed community. Accountability. Fellowship. Friends. Family.

You need the same.

Find others who are learning to finish faithfully. Walk with them. Share struggles. Celebrate victories. Hold each other accountable.

The Rhythm of Finishing

Once you've chosen your quest and committed to the complete 3-Phase Follow Through, establish rhythms that support finishing:

Daily Rhythm: PHASE 2 (DO)

Show up for the work. One focused hour on your dream doing quest (or whatever amount of time works for you). One physical discipline to stay strong. One relationship to invest in. All while staying connected to God through Bible study and prayer.

Weekly Rhythm: PHASE 3 (REAP) AND PHASE 1 (DREAM)

Debrief: Review the week. What did you learn? What worked? What didn't?

Rest: One full day off from work (Sabbath). Rest intentionally.

Reap Rewards: Celebrate progress. Acknowledge victories. Receive transformation.

Then dream by setting targets for the coming week.

Project Rhythm: Complete All 3 Phases

Don't start the next thing until you've finished THIS thing. Not just crossed the finish line but completed the whole cycle through PHASE 3: REAP.

Yearly Rhythm: Stack Complete Cycles

Stack faithful days, weeks, and projects. Each completion creates capacity for what's next. Each cycle compounds transformation.

This isn't about speed. It's about thoroughness. God took 4,000 years to prepare the world for Christ. Patience isn't passive. It's powerful.

Finishing Isn't Crossing the Finish Line

I thought finishing meant crossing the finish line. I was wrong.

After the marathon, I crossed the finish line but felt empty.

After my first novel, I didn't believe I accomplished anything important enough to share.

After the 101 Day Challenge, I completed the task but didn't complete the transformation.

Because I stopped at PHASE 2 (DO) and skipped PHASE 3 (REAP).

The work was done, but I was still the same person who just accomplished something. I hadn't become someone new.

Finishing isn't crossing the finish line. Finishing is completing all 3 phases.

DREAM → DO → REAP. Then DREAM AGAIN from new capacity.

The cycle never ends. But each cycle transforms you. And each transformation makes you more like Christ.

That's the invisible mission. That's what matters most.

Live Boldly

The God who planned redemption before the foundation of the world, worked for 4,000 years to prepare the world for Christ, and finished the work of salvation on the cross is the same God walking with you right now.

He finishes what He starts.

Including you.

"For it is God who is working in you both to will and to work according to His good purpose" (Philippians 2:13).

So answer the call. Choose your quest. Walk through all 3 phases. Expect resistance at your fade phase. Join a fellowship of finishers.

And remember: you're not managing projects. You're living an epic adventure that reveals who God is through who you're becoming.

Your struggles are character development.

Your dreams are invitations to deeper fellowship.

Your battles reveal God's power.

Your transformation points others to Christ.

Now go be the warrior He designed you to be.

Live your adventure boldly.

Finish your quest faithfully.

And trust the God who never quits.

Dream. Do. Follow Through.

Reap the rewards God has for you.

In Christ,

Bonnie Jean

About the Author

BONNIE JEAN SCHAEFER IS the Adventurous Author who adventurizes life.

She's on a mission to anchor Christians in who God is so they know who they are — and then live boldly from that place. Her framework? **Start with WHO. And WHO starts with God.**

A lifelong Christian with a Bible degree from Cedarville College (now Cedarville University), Bonnie hosts *The Adventurous Author* podcast and founded Dream Doers Publishing. She writes under her own name for faith and writing content and as D.K. Drake for the *Dragon Stalker Bloodlines* fantasy saga.

The same woman who's crossed five marathon finish lines and tackled 50K trail races approaches faith with equal intensity. She lives in North Carolina with her two sisters, raising four adopted children and proving that anchored people live adventurously as Dream Doers.

The 50 by 50 Mission

Bonnie is publishing 50 books by her 50th birthday. The mission started on her 48th birthday to challenge her to finish books in various stages of the writing process: *The Faithful Christian Living Experience* (12 foundational books), *The Wealthy Writer Experience* (training for God's creatives), and 35+ children's stories through the *Everrlyn Experience* and *Zella Zeal Experience*.

This is book 3 of 50.

Join the adventure at TheAdventurousAuthor.com/league for monthly storytelling tournaments, weekly sparks, and the digital version of every book as it releases — just $7/month.

What adventure is God prompting YOU to start?

WHY THIS SERIES EXISTS

THE FAITHFUL CHRISTIAN LIVING EXPERIENCE

DEAR READER,

I am not writing these books because I have all the answers. I'm writing them because I have all the questions.

I wanted answers to my questions, so I studied Bible in college and kept digging long after I earned that degree. I gained solid theological knowledge. But knowledge alone wasn't enough.

I could live it with quiet conviction, but I couldn't synthesize it. I couldn't articulate it with clarity. And I didn't have the boldness to speak up and speak out in a way God was calling me to.

So a few years ago, I wanted to distill everything I'd learned from Scripture into a framework that felt like a story rather than systematic theology — a framework I could actually live and speak from, not just study. I wanted to connect the dots in a way that anchored my soul, fueled my faith, and helped me related to my God effectively.

So I started pray-thinking in my journal, wrestling with the foundational questions every Christian needs to answer:

- **Who is God?** What is He like? What makes Him unique?

- **Who is God in relation to me?** Is He distant? Engaged? What does it mean that He calls Himself Creator, King, Judge, Savior, Father, Friend, and Helper?

- **What does God want, and why?** What are His driving purposes, and how does He accomplish them?

- **Why should I trust the Bible?** What makes it different from every other religious text? In a world of noise and deception, how do I know what's real?

- **What happens after I die?** Is eternity real or just a comforting story?

- **Who is Satan?** What does my greatest enemy want, and how does he try to get it?

- **Why do I matter?** What's my purpose in God's eternal plan?

- **How did God design me?** What does it mean to be made in His image — heart, mind, body, and soul?

- **How do I live from this foundation?** What values guide me? What's my character foundation? How do I set goals that honor God?

The Faithful Christian Living Experience books are the result of that wrestling. They are designed to give you a framework for knowing God, understanding yourself, and living faithfully in a world that's hostile to truth.

These 11 catalyst books are designed to anchor your faith:

- **Anchored Faith** (Books 1-3) — Know God, Trust God, Walk with God

- **Anchored Truth** (Books 4-6) — Explore why the Bible is true, the reality of eternity, and your invisible enemy (and how to fight him effectively)

- **Anchored Identity** (Books 7-8) — Discover who you are in Christ and why you are significant

- **Anchored Living** (Books 9-11) — Walk out what you've learned in a way that aligns with God and your design

These aren't theology textbooks. They're conversations with God about identity: His, mine, and yours. Each book builds on the foundation laid before it, because you can't discern truth without first knowing God. You know who you are without building on TRUTH. You can't live effectively without knowing who you are IN CHRIST.

This is the hard work of building unshakeable faith that withstands storms, resists deception, and finishes what God starts.

You'll never reach the end of knowing God. He's infinite, and you're finite. But that's makes seeking Him a thrilling adventure — one that carries through from this life into eternity.

And you don't have to walk this journey alone.

In Christ,

Bonnie Jean Schaefer

P.S. I'd love to hear how this book has impacted your relationship with God. Please share your story as an email to me (bonnie@adventurizelife.com) or as a review on Amazon.

Join the Adventure at TheAdventuruousAuthor.com.

THE LEAGUE OF ADVENTUROUS AUTHORS

FOR YEARS, I CALLED myself an "aspiring writer." I had the calling. I had the faith. I had stories burning in my bones.

But I couldn't finish anything.

Random writing bursts. Broken promises. Guilt every time I chose writing over family time. The loop of starting projects and abandoning them at Chapter 3.

That's why I built **The League of Adventurous Authors™**—because I needed the flexible lifestyle system rooted in Christ I couldn't find anywhere else.

It's a Christ-anchored training league that fixes **Creative Identity first** (just like this book anchored you in who God is and who you are in Him), then builds the rhythm that actually lasts.

If you're a Christian fiction author ready to:

– Stop calling yourself "aspiring"

– Write consistently without guilt

– Finish stories you start

– Train for faithfulness, not fame

– ENJOY the process of doing hard things...

Join me in The League at TheAdventurousAuthor.com/league or listen to The Adventurous Author podcast.

Let's train together.

—Bonnie Jean